Past in Mind

A Heritage Project
and
Mental Health Recovery

Katherine Lack

Published by the Author

© Katherine Lack 2014

ISBN = 978-0-9546212-4-7

Set in 10pt Arial and printed in England by Orphans Press Ltd., Arrow Close, Leominster Enterpise Park, Leominster, Herefordshire HR6 0LD.

'. . . the historian of the family . . . must recognise three duties: . . . first to his own generation, second to people in the past and third . . . to search after the truth. [We have] a citizen's role as accredited experts, to whom those concerned with welfare, with social solidarity and with mutual support, can turn for information. . . . We are bound to try to understand the situation, attitudes and actions [of people in the past] in their own terms as well as in our own. . . . Once we acknowledge that our obligation as historians is to the interests and aims of everyone who lived before our day and in our day as well, we [are] faced with the principle of behaviour that . . . the everyday emotions and customary desires of the ordinary persons of former generations, every single one of them, have an urgent claim on our attention.'

Peter Laslett

(in: 'The Character of Familial History, its Limitations and the Conditions for its Proper Pursuit', *Journal of Family History* 12 (1987): 263-84)

Contents

page

Acknowledgements ii

Glossary iii

Foreword 1

Chapter 1: The Past in Mind Project: Recovering Lives in a Studmarsh
Landscape 4

Chapter 2: What's in a Name? 12

Chapter 3: On the Margins 23

Chapter 4: People in the Landscape 32

Chapter 5: The Mind of the Past: Trauma and Recovery 39

Chapter 6: New Hope and A New Outlook 51

Chapter 7: A Day in the Life of Past in Mind 69

Text Figures

Figure 1: An Approximate Time Line of Herefordshire from Prehistory
to 1066 12

Figure 2: A Map of the Parishes near Studmarsh, with their Iron Age Forts 13

Figure 3: The Maximum Extent of the Kingdom of Ergyng 25

Figure 4: The Site Area, on the Linton, Norton and Whitbourne Boundaries 26

Figure 5: Neighbouring Properties Relating to the Studmarsh Story 53

Figure 6: The Colley Family Tree 56

Figure 7: The Early Part of the Biddle Family Tree 58

Figure 8: The Later Part of the Biddle Family Tree 61

Acknowledgements

This book arose out of the Past in Mind Project, which was the brain-child of Jenny McMillan and Ian Bapty. Without them, needless to say, none of it would have happened: they developed the concept, applied for the funding and set up the structures to make the project work. It has been a privilege to get to know them both, and in particular to work with Jenny, who was Project Manager and has subsequently been my valued collaborator in the production of the book. Chapter One is largely her work, although I am wholly responsible for its final form.

That Past in Mind was such a success is testament to many people who gave their time and expertise, in a whole variety of different ways. It was a multi-faceted project, and consequently it is, sadly, impossible to list all those who contributed. What follows is only a bare outline, and while I know that all those individuals who were involved feel that their participation was fruitful, I regret that they are not all mentioned specifically here. I only joined the project at a relatively late stage of its development, and am no doubt unaware of much of the groundwork that was done.

The archaeological work has already been written up as a report by Dai Williams and Chris Atkinson, who were the lead field archaeologists: I have drawn extensively on their work, and apologise if I have misinterpreted any of their conclusions. Without their inspirational and generous contribution, the project would not have succeeded, as is apparent from the participants' comments quoted here.

My role during the project was to lead the historical training programme and research. A large number of people took part, of whom Claire Rush and Steve Palmer, and Judith Evans, Deborah Jarman, Margaret Morris and Di Stephenson from the Bromyard History Society, were particularly invaluable. I hope that they can represent all the others, too numerous to name.

When writing the book itself, I have greatly appreciated the help of Rhys Griffiths and the staff at the Hereford Record Office, for assistance with locating some of the early wills, and Victoria Bryant at the Worcestershire Archaeology Unit for her efforts to find pictures of representative pottery specimens. Several people have helped with reading early drafts of the text, especially Jenny McMillan, Claire Rush and my long-suffering husband; Professor Derek Smith and Dr Matt Edwards also read several chapters, and all these people made valued contributions.

Specific picture credits are given where appropriate; where there are none, the pictures were taken by my husband Paul, to whom I can only extend my most grateful thanks as always.

The real success of the project was due to its participants, be they professionals, amateurs, beginners or experts. It has been a great pleasure for me to get to know so many new people in the course of the project, and I trust that this book is in some sense a reflection of the triumph that was Past in Mind.

Glossary

assart: land or fields taken in from commons or woodland and cleared for agriculture.

commons: areas of unfarmed manorial land, regulated and used for rough grazing, pig fattening, wood collection etc.

cruck: medieval method of construction, using pairs of timbers cut from a curving tree to make the principal frames of a house. By the sixteenth century most new buildings were being made with square frames, using vertical corner posts.

customary holding: tenants who owed locally-defined duties to the lord of the manor, in addition to money payments; many were obliged to work for specified hours on the lord's land.

ældorman: high-status Anglo-Saxon nobleman, many of whom were entrusted with ruling a shire. In the eleventh century the rank became equated with the earls.

free holding: a higher-status land-holding, with fewer obligations to the lord apart from a money payment. By the eighteenth century, manorial obligations were becoming nominal on even the most traditional manors, and the requirement to pay tithes (one tenth of the produce of the land) to support the parish priest was a source of much greater vexation and resentment.

hearth tax: one of the measures aimed at raising much-needed revenue after the Civil Wars. Levied between 1662 and 1689/90 at 2s. per hearth on all but the poorest households, they were always unpopular because inspectors could force entry into private homes and because there were so many recently-built fireplaces and chimneys. Hearth taxes were replaced by the window tax.

hide: a land unit, varying from about 40 acres to 120, based in part on the number of people a given area could support. In Herefordshire it probably corresponded to about 120 acres.

hundred: the local administrative unit, perhaps originally based on 100 hides.

joyne: wooden furniture, such as chests, made with joinery-work.

Lent grain: spring-sown cereal crops, especially wheat.

manor: an estate with its land divided into that worked by the tenants for their lord (the demesne) and the remainder in small plots worked by the tenants for themselves. After the Norman Conquest, land in England was explicitly owned by the king, with tenants-in-chief (such as Roger de Lacy) and sub-tenants holding manors from him. Manors were often co-terminous with a village, but some included many settlements, while larger parishes could have two or more manors.

mental health recovery: unlike 'clinical' recovery, which assumes that a patient will eventually be cured of their symptoms by the expertise of a professional, and will 'get back to normal', the recovery model focuses on the strengths and expertise of the individual in a more holistic way. It involves the development of new meaning, purpose and hope in one's life, and encourages those with mental health problems to be pro-active in shaping their future, by means of a wide range of networks rather than exclusively mental health agencies.

mark: a sum of money worth 13s.4d. There were three half-marks in a pound.

minster: a mother church, often dating back to the eighth century or even earlier, with several priests who served the surrounding countryside.

money: the old money system was based on a silver penny, 12 of which made a shilling and 240 (20 shillings) a pound, with 240 standard pennies weighing one pound. Neither shilling nor pound coins existed until modern times; instead, calculations were based on marks and half marks.

noble: a gold coin, valued in the late medieval period at 6s.8d., or half a mark.

palimpsest: a parchment which has been re-used. With care, the earlier text can be deciphered below the surface writing.

shire court: the main unit of justice in Anglo-Saxon England, to which the local hundred courts (which met monthly) reported. The shires eventually became the counties.

thegn: in Anglo-Saxon law, a holder of land by military service; hence a minor aristocrat.

thrum: a thick cloth with a fringe of tassels or loose threads.

virgate: a land unit smaller than a hide; in Herefordshire, generally about 30 acres (a quarter of a hide).

yeoman: a farmer, typically a freeholder of a relatively small acreage but enough to permit a voice in local politics, social welfare and justice. In Herefordshire, the yeomen remained a cultural force until well into the nineteenth century.

Past in Mind — Foreword

This is a fascinating book about a remarkable project. The project is an intriguing interplay between archaeological and historical investigation and ideas about 'recovery' in mental health. The research was led by professionals but many of the workers were volunteers living with or recovering from mental health problems. The result was a complex, shared journey of discovery with continual explorations of historical, psychological and social themes. At the beginning it is stated that, *'Archaeology is fundamentally about understanding people and human experience … through study of the physical evidence of the past'*. This book strives to fill in the gaps around these historical artefacts with personal and psychological meaning and insights into the social lives and communities of the people who lived in Studmarsh from earliest times to the eighteenth century.

The links between the processes of historical study and recovery in mental health are many and various. In the first place, both involve telling stories. Archaeological stories are woven around physical evidence from the past; our human stories are pieced together from the remembered fragments of our lives as we struggle to assemble them into a coherent and meaningful narrative. This is why stories are so important in recovery (Roberts, G. (2000) Narrative and severe mental illness: what place do stories have in an evidence-based world? *Advances in Psychiatric Treatment*, **6**, 432-441). Like archaeology, recovery is based on carefully handling and analysing one's own past in order to live better in the present.

Secondly – and this often follow from the process of constructing our story – recovery is about finding a different relationship between ourselves and our problems. The traditional relationship between people and their problems in mental health is that we *are* our problems; we don't just own them, we are defined by them and we often feel lost inside them waiting to be rescued by some omniscient professional or powerful medicine. Recovery gives us a different way of thinking about these experiences. It is based on a notion that our mental experiences are just a <u>part</u> of us – an important part maybe – but we also have many other different and rich identities. We are not just 'a schizophrenic' or 'a depressive', we are a *person* with psychotic or depressive symptoms, able to respond and, to some extent, control our experiences or, if necessary, live with them and learn to manage them while we pursue our lives. This is evident in the book as we learn about the different characters of the volunteers.

We are therefore warned repeatedly against 'labelling' people and drawing conclusions based on very imperfect knowledge - a salutary lesson for any ambitious professional interested in usefully supporting people on their personal recovery journey.

The style of the project, with 'volunteers' operating on an equal level with professional archaeologists and historians, also clearly gave the volunteers a powerful sense of their own ability to make a contribution and their own worth as individuals. This is apparent from the testimonies of some of the workers:

I feel privileged to be a volunteer. This is giving me the chance to make a genuine contribution - to the National Archive, to the local community, to our group. I am spurred on by this thought, and I know that the other volunteers are driven in a similar way. I cannot help feeling exhilarated and optimistic. This feels really, really good.

This experience is very similar to the comments made by people attending the new 'Recovery Colleges' (McGregor, Repper & Brown (2014) "The college is so different from anything I have done": A study of the characteristics of Nottingham Recovery College, *Journal of Mental Health Education, Training and Practice*, **9**, 3-15). They discover a place where they can *learn* about living with mental health problems with professionals and service users working together on an equal basis, each bringing different expertise to the endeavour. They find this liberating and empowering, enhancing their sense of control over themselves and their lives. This seems exactly the same as the experiences of the volunteers on Past in Mind.

Thirdly, at the heart of recovery is the process of coming to terms with trauma. We all experience trauma in our lives and, for most of us, it is an experience that we learn from both in terms of how we cope 'internally' and also what kinds of external supports are most helpful to us in times of trouble. Rural England in the fourteenth and fifteenth centuries was certainly full of trauma – death, poverty, unemployment, disputes between families and neighbours, difficult relationships, unreasonable 'employers', etc. – and it is therefore not surprising that people in those days experienced very similar symptoms of mental distress to those we recognise today (McDonald, M. (1983) *'Mystical Bedlam – Madness, Anxiety and Healing in Seventeenth century England'*, Cambridge Studies in the History of Medicine: Cambridge University Press). However, as McDonald's book makes clear, although people experienced familiar signs and symptoms of mental distress, the meanings they attached to them – and the remedies they used to 'treat' them – were very different.

In this account we get a strong sense of the impact of one particular trauma – that of the Black Death. Its consequences were truly 'apocalyptic', with between a quarter and a third of the population wiped out. The likely psychological social impact of these events is well described by one of the volunteers:

Everyone living in Studmarsh would have lost a loved one or maybe a whole family, friends, neighbours. There would be little time to indulge grief, because the need to survive would be uppermost in your thoughts. Fear for your own life and that of others close to you would never go away. Lawlessness and the ripping of social fabric would leave you helpless. Every man for himself! There was a sense of tragedy in Studmarsh during the dig as we uncovered the layers of stones and the layers of people's lives, fragments of pottery, stones from a building. We felt close to the humans of the past. Would the grief and fear prevalent during the waves of the Black Death have united people? Would there have been any solidarity, as there was during the dig when everyone was together in the rain in the field? Would individuals experiencing grief and depression have taken comfort from the shared experience, possible understanding or advice from other people?

These words echo the experiences of many people today as they struggle to recover from less catastrophic, but equally upsetting, life events. But, we can end our discussion of the Black Death on an optimistic note, since out of the trauma and disasters of the fourteenth century, a new community gradually emerged. *'The survivors became adaptors and innovators, working at new ways of living, just as those adapting to life with a disability are, although few may know it, among the most creative and proactive members of our communities today'*.

The final theme which reads clearly across from the historical investigations to ideas about recovery and mental health today is that of the need to overcome feelings of alienation and to be a part of society again. History – and life – is about coping with change and in many instances the implications of change for peoples' sense of belonging is strikingly highlighted. For example, what was it like for the Saxons in the early years when few of their neighbours would have understood them or looked kindly on them? Or, what was it like for the British in the eleventh century when their land was taken over by new rulers, speaking in another unfamiliar language? Did the first Norman settlers also *feel* isolated and vulnerable? These emotional questions ring down the corridors of history.

For all people at all times there is a creative synthesis between mental well-being and social inclusion. Recovery requires social inclusion and social inclusion helps to promote recovery. In the case of the 'Past in Mind' project the two come together in a mutually reinforcing paradigm that offers people with mental health issues a route to rejoin society on an equal basis thereby promoting their mental health.

Above all this is an absorbing book. The scholarship is serious, but the tone is always light and engaging. It is never too solemn or technical. Indeed, sometimes it plays with the central interaction between the ancient and the modern (e.g. one volunteer's 'Blog from the Bog'!). Nevertheless, it is wonderful example of inter-disciplinary study. The subject of history and the subject of trying to understand and help people with mental distress are both subtle and complicated and open to multiple interpretations. We therefore need as many different tools to study these phenomena as we can get hold of. This is one example of a new collaboration. Hopefully, it won't be the last.

Professor Geoff Shepherd
ImROC Recovery Programme Lead, Centre for Mental Health, London
March 2014

Chapter 1. The Past in Mind Project: Recovering Lives in a Studmarsh Landscape

This book is about a remarkable heritage project. It is about how history and archaeology can tell a story of a place and its people, but it is also about mental health recovery and the emerging personal journeys of men and women through the centuries, and the universal strands that impact on us all as humans.[1]

The Past in Mind project was a novel concept from the outset. It sought to use the disciplines of archaeology and history to investigate the past while enabling people with mental health problems to create a new narrative for themselves beyond illness. It is based on the idea of a natural synergy or correlation between the painstaking discipline that uncovers evidence of the past, and mental health recovery which relies upon the careful handling, analysis and ordering of one's own past in order to live better in the present.

We believe that the Past in Mind project is a success simply because it happened at all. The mental health charity Herefordshire Mind applied for and received the funding from the Heritage Lottery Fund (HLF) to run a project that would include a full archaeological and historical investigation of our site in Studmarsh meadow, Herefordshire. But there was no blue-print or prototype for such a dual-based project, so its successful outcomes are testament to the strength of the model and to the commitment of the team of volunteers and specialists.

So what was the model and how did it determine what happened?

The concept evolved out of discussions that took place between an archaeologist and a mental health practitioner. Both were concerned with people, how they live and how we understand 'their' past. By using metaphors like 'digging into the past' or finding the 'bedrock' of our existence an idea emerged which eventually became the Past in Mind project. Metaphor is sometimes used in therapy with powerful effect; by its very nature it can help to transfer new meaning or act as a bridge to deeper understanding that more conscious 'talking therapy' may not provide. In this case, the heart of the project was being able to link the investigation of the heritage of a place called Studmarsh with the more personal heritage of those presently living with mental health difficulties. In essence, one could examine the complexities of one's own life and history at one step removed, by digging into the past of others. We could thus realise the aim of 'positively placing past in mind':

> Archaeology is fundamentally about understanding people and human experience but it does so in a context of study (the physical evidence of the past) whose apparent distance from immediate personal, community and social agendas makes this difficult topic attractive, accessible, inclusive and comfortable.[2]

---

1 see Glossary for a definition of mental health recovery
2 Ian Bapty, Senior Archaeologist, *pers.comm.*

Although it was this theory and the inter-disciplinary synergy that first ignited our interest, it is important to remember that Past in Mind was and is fundamentally a heritage project. The funding came from HLF and we had to meet a raft of specific objectives and outcomes, in heritage terms. It was how and by what means those objectives were achieved that continued to set the project apart, as it relied heavily upon the establishment of a sound value base and rigorous attention to inclusive principles. What did this means in real terms? Basically, it needed to be a community heritage project owned by all those taking part and resting on the premise that there would be a two-way learning process for all concerned. It was agreed that there would be no demarcation, so apart from the archaeologists and the historian, everyone else taking part would be a volunteer. Having a level playing field set the tone and also fitted with the Personal Recovery Framework, whereby wellbeing is enhanced through the development of a positive identity and valued social roles. Past in Mind offered a more subtle opportunity where volunteers who had not experienced or been labelled with mental health problems could work alongside other volunteers 'like themselves'. In this way, relationships were formed, fears eroded and barriers broken down. This drew upon the key tenets of the recovery model in mental health which suggest that only genuine inclusion can produce change, purpose and renewed confidence. During the excavation there was a fair bit of 'getting down and dirty' together, and nobody, not even the 'experts', knew in advance what would be discovered.

The project aimed at 'a creative synthesis between recovery and social inclusion; recovery both requires and allows social inclusion and social inclusion helps to promote recovery.'[3] Inclusion targets the impact of stigma and discrimination which is prevalent when people are seen to be 'different'. That difference can come from being labelled as dysfunctional, weak or even dangerous, which in turn often leads to stigma. This can arise in two interwoven ways. Social stigma is characterised by prejudicial attitudes and behaviour directed at individuals because of the 'psychiatric' label. Equally seriously, perceived stigma is the internalization of that stigma: the person 'takes it on' and so the cycle continues. Opportunity lessens through stigma and low expectations. Cultural and social labels like these are part and parcel of our national history, and Chapter 2 explores this historical dimension and reminds us that people do get trapped in their names and the history they carry. The names used of the past also reflect and impact on our understanding and acceptance of it. Labels and the inherent consequences can stick. We make assumptions about history, just as we are capable of doing this about a person and their personal narrative.

Our project also showed that Studmarsh is a place that sits on the margins, a place apart and yet a place where so much history lay hidden beneath. Similarly, people who have experienced trauma, loss, abuse or stress may be affected in such a way that they feel marginalised. The need to feel part of things is crucial in maintaining balance and perspective but the sense of being on the outside alienates and sets apart. Traumatic experience shatters basic personal and cultural assumptions about the primary way we order reality; the future is no longer

3 Social Inclusion Scoping Group Royal College of Psychiatrists, *Making Psychiatry and Mental Health Services Fit for the 21st Century: Mental Health and Social Inclusion*2009 [cited]; available from www.rcpsych.ac.uk/pdf/Ps01_2009x.pdf

predictable and because of dissociation, the past is no longer known. Chapter 5 in particular is about trauma and how the events of the fourteenth century go far beyond the apocalyptic loss of life. We no longer have the plague, but the cries of lost communities and dislocated lives still echo down the centuries, in stigma and fear of misunderstood 'others'.

The very nature of the project was defined by margins, both internal and external, but sometimes the margins can become a place of growth. Just as the comments, annotations and scribbles in the margins of early documents can reveal much about the lives of those reading them centuries ago, so the margins and the people who find themselves there are important themes in this project. The opportunity was to learn the value of their contributions 'in the margins'. Through the three-way boundary between past lives, the past of contemporary lives and present living, the project managed in the process to weave a strong bond between the volunteers and people from the past.

Chapter 3 explores a number of questions about barriers, in both a historical and social context. The parish boundaries on Bringsty Common, which run close to our meadow, would have represented security and an assertion of rights not available to those on the other side. There are analogies here with the debates on security versus freedom, and the relative merits of institutionalised living versus care and residence in the community, even maybe the arguments about the porosity of national borders. Do barriers make people feel safe, and if so, are they for the benefit of people inside or outside?

As we know, heritage is not a 'fact', it is an idea and an interpretation. The official version of the past is not set in stone, and being able to put an interpretation on the heritage we uncovered was fundamental.

> Not to be inclusive of different perceptions and narratives risks making the past accessible only to those who can afford it, those who go along with narratives that do nothing to challenge the self-imposed superiority of the 'established' order. . . Archaeology is political by definition because it involves at some level the prioritisation of one narrative, one way of 'telling the past' over others. If along with providing insight into our deeper shared past, archaeology can aid cohesion and concurrently help enhance 'belongingness' in the present, so much the better.[4]

How a project gets underway is crucial to its success. In laying the foundations for Past in Mind it was vital that the local community and the relevant organisations were on board and not only clear about what they could offer but also what the project aimed for in terms of cross-fertilization of ideas and learning. Otherwise the experience for the individual participants would have been eroded. Archaeological and historical investigation into our past fascinates many people as we can see from programmes like 'Time Team'. By drawing on that natural curiosity and interest in local history, the project ignited enthusiasm and excitement. We enlisted the support and resources of many groups in Herefordshire who had a

---

4 R Kiddey and J Schofield, 'Embrace the Margins: Adventures in Archaeology and Homelessness', *Public Archaeology* 10 (2011): 4-22, pp. 185 & 189

particular interest in Studmarsh, the place and its people. The National Trust at Lower Brockhampton Estate, The Bromyard and District Local History Society and Herefordshire Nature Trust all embraced the project. The cross-community appeal of such disciplined investigation made it an ideal activity for engaging the interest of people from different backgrounds. A striking feature of the project was its ability to attract and sustain involvement from a diverse range of people. Students from colleges, university graduates, retired business managers and teachers, builders, bird-watchers and local farm workers – all became volunteers.

Past in Mind asked that people learn from each other. How this might work in practice, we did not know. What new understandings would come from one discipline being exposed to another? What might 'the experts' gain from novice amateurs? Would the development of new relationships bring about change? What cross-fertilization of ideas would emerge and what insights might give rise to hope and transformation? The Past in Mind model rests on inclusive principles but with the recognition that everyone is different. It was therefore important from a project management point of view not to be prescriptive but to allow people to take risks, to challenge themselves and to fail if necessary. This process required a profound understanding of the aims and objectives and what they had set out to achieve. It also demanded discretion and a deep appreciation for the risks that were being taken by everyone in stepping out of their own particular comfort zone.

The original 'spark' or premise for this project came from an analogy with archaeology, with 'what lay below the surface'. The historical research was then instrumental in 'bringing to life' the forgotten people of a small community, through learning the skills of research and understanding what constitutes evidence. This again was in tune with personal analysis in mental health recovery. The programme of historical activities, including visits to museums and the county and local record centres, ran alongside the survey, excavation and cataloguing. And it has continued, drawing together the story in this book. By using the two disciplines to uncover the historical events, the whole experience was more holistic and with greater opportunity for depth of learning. Conversely it was also challenging as the two fields brought different and often conflicting slants to the understanding of the past. This allowed us to ask questions, to reflect, to reassess our assumptions, to start from opposing positions, to respect but differ, to draw contrary conclusions, to want to know more and to be left with more questions than answers. Working within these tensions was a vital part of the project, since there are so many ways to interpret the significance and the impact of events on people and their world. This helped us to draw out the differences between the medical and recovery models in mental health, psychiatry and psychology, with their divergent views of the role of the 'expert'. By applying the critical analysis and deduction needed for the Past in Mind disciplines, volunteers fed into the process and brought the themes outlined in the rest of this book to life. The key to this was in the skill and facilitative qualities of the relevant specialists, who appreciated the need to demystify the aura around professional research while giving volunteers permission to have a view or an interpretation on the meaning of evidence that was emerging. But it also depended on the willingness of volunteers with a wide range of experience to make their own contributions. By consistently drawing on the strengths of the volunteer team, momentum and confidence grew, further breaking down barriers and exposing some of the myths of mental illness.

Mental health recovery is about a personal journey, developing new meaning and purpose in one's individual life even while living to the limits imposed by illness. The over-riding analogy that emerged through the project was that the people of this particular place in times past were also constrained by their circumstances. Their individual lives and the meaning they placed on the landscape became a major theme, which is explored in Chapters 4 and 6. We began to see how culturally, socially and sometimes emotionally loaded this can be, because interpretation varies according to who and where you are. For the rich, the mobile and the free a certain place may well be associated with wealth and leisure, while for a medieval farming community, life on the land must have been largely defined by the cycle of the seasons. In the wet summer of 2012, Past in Mind volunteers became 'people of the land' walking in the footsteps of the men, women and children of Studmarsh who lived there through the centuries. Being able to name people brought individuals and their stories to life, while the historical documents illuminated the struggles and hardships they faced from famine, poverty or persecution. Society was far from equitable and examining how power and powerlessness played out at junctures over a thousand year period resonated with many. Volunteers were able to draw comparisons with their own situations at times both from an economic and social point of view; there were resonances with mental ill-health in particular, with its tendency to label someone as incapable, worthless or socially ineffectual. The disciplines of archaeological and historical research both played distinct roles role in humanising Studmarsh, until it was no longer just a place of measurement, meadow or statistics. Instead, it became a society of individuals in their family and community context.

Out of times of historical trauma came a healthier period, with new opportunities brought about by human resourcefulness. Likewise through the Past in Mind process volunteers emerged as individuals with particular views, skills and humour. They became people with families, like those we met in the archives. And so the opportunities that the project provided for all volunteers lay not only in the realm of heritage. 'Getting your eye in' (to use an archaeological term) refers to the observation, discernment and critical analysis necessary for making informed judgements about the emerging patterns during excavation. These skills were transferred and applied to other aspects of the project and to the personal lives of volunteers. Meanwhile, the resourcefulness of the past residents of Studmarsh was mirrored in a wealth of creativity, including film-making, photography, poetry, drawing, and the 'Day in the Life' celebration at the end. There is no doubt that the design and the 'feel' of the project was conducive to self-expression, but the place itself and the natural environment around Studmarsh also provided its own kind of space for reflection. Eco-therapists describe this as the 'nurture' that promotes a mutual connection between the external and internal. With Herefordshire Nature Trust collaborating in the project, volunteers were afforded a structured opportunity to be more involved with this dimension as well.

And Now . . . A View of Past in Mind from Two Volunteers.

One of the participants said simply that it had been the best year of her life. Even though the project is over and mental health problems remain, she continues to draw on the knowledge, skills and contacts made during that time. The very fact that it happened and it fulfilled a dream from childhood means that she now has hope, and a renewed confidence that change can happen.

Claire Rush, who was both a volunteer and part of the planning team, has written:

> From the outset we decided that all participants would be volunteers, and this limited categorising people. For many people who may be mental health service users being a volunteer demonstrated that this was a valuable research project breaking away from traditional occupational therapy. There was something hugely positive about being part of a task-force which was, in effect, about to make history.

> The project combined historical research, a full-scale archaeological excavation, and several community workshops where all those involved were encouraged to put forward ideas and ask questions. We had lots of public open days to raise awareness and encourage participation, and the final symposium at the end of the project, in spring 2013, took place at Bromyard Conquest Theatre. Many volunteers (some wearing period costume) took part in a staged performance reciting 'Day in the Life' monologues written to capture different aspects of the project. As a member of the project team I set up a Blog for Past in Mind[5] to convey the spirit of the project. I hoped that volunteers would feel confident enough to write about their experiences of working on the project. I did not anticipate that the Blog would become the project noticeboard, as well as being a place where some volunteers felt able to describe their past experiences in the context of the project. Consequently the Blog frequently changed shape and direction, while ebbing and flowing with the course of Past in Mind itself. The very fact that the Blog was established and monitored by volunteers is another example of how the inclusive principles laid down at the outset played out in reality. The Blog was our window to the world while acting as a base camp for ideas and expression. Photographs taken by fellow volunteers were displayed so events in the life of the project were catalogued and celebrated.

> As a former Classics student I was thrilled to delve into the parish records which were written in medieval Latin. Medieval Latin is less fastidious than classical Latin and I had not translated it before, but once I became more accustomed to it I felt its immediacy and a consequent connection with the people of the time. In particular the records of the parish of Cradley had a profound effect on me. The Latin text conveyed the torn social fabric and general decay following the Black Death. Lawlessness, dubious clerics, broken and neglected buildings, all

---

5 http://pastinmindproject.wordpress.com/

screamed of human tragedy and chaos. The horrific impact of the Black Death slammed into me as I was trying to translate some of the text. In translation this impact was inevitably diluted, so I felt enormously privileged to be given a glimpse into the 14th century despite it being very chilling.

Black Death and Black Dog! The impact of the Black Death on ordinary people! Everyone living in Studmarsh would have lost a loved one or maybe a whole family, friends, neighbours. There would be little time to indulge grief, because the need to survive would be uppermost in your thoughts. Fear for your own life and that of others close to you would never go away. Lawlessness and the ripping of social fabric would leave you helpless. Every man for himself! There was a sense of tragedy in Studmarsh during the dig as we uncovered the layers of stones and the layers of people's lives, fragments of pottery, stones from a building. We felt close to the humans of the past. Would the grief and fear prevalent during the waves of the Black Death have united people? Would there have been any solidarity, as there was during the dig when everyone was together in the rain in the field? Would individuals experiencing grief and depression have taken comfort from the shared experience, possible understanding or advice from other people? The good side of human nature in a shared crisis (compassion, assistance, and selflessness) and the bad side of human nature (looting, lawlessness, and intimidation) would have both been exaggerated. How would people have dealt with the black dog? Drink? Looting? Talking? Music? Religion? Violence? Or would they not have had time or energy or the space to even acknowledge it?

Perhaps this insight into the Black Death heightened my awareness during the excavation, because I could not hold a fragment of pottery or a building stone without thinking of the human beings who had once been connected to them. All the volunteers who took part in the excavation were mindful of this to some extent, especially as it became clear that the site had seen a catastrophic population decline in the 14th century.

The excavation was the raw and physical part of Past in Mind which has imprinted the summer of 2012 on many volunteers' memories. The camaraderie, physical exertion, fresh air, anticipation and focus kept everyone going for weeks. Recovering of artefacts was like recovering lost memories from our own past. Part of mental health recovery is about understanding ourselves and often we can do that through learning about others. Finding out what makes us all human, what links us together as a species or as part of an evolving process helps give us a sense of purpose and meaning.

At the end of the excavation period the backfilling process enabled people to return stones and soil layer by layer until the field bore little trace of our intrusion. The mental health recovery process has parallels with this on several levels, and some volunteers were able to analyse it in some depth in relation to their own lives which is very much in keeping with the original concept.

The excavation was extremely intense and high-spirited, which left a gaping hole afterwards. Some volunteers struggled to adjust to ordinary life after the two weeks in the field in particular, as it felt like coming back down to earth with a bang. However this sense of loss must be seen in proportion as no one would disagree that while Team GB were excelling in the Summer 2012 Olympics, Team Past in Mind were also achieving success and making history in the Studmarsh meadow.

Chapter 2. What's in a Name?

Does it matter what we call things? Should we be concerned about what labels are attached to particular people, things or events? Juliet thought it didn't matter, but as Shakespeare reminds us, names are all too important. The tragedy of Romeo and Juliet was that they were trapped in their names, the labels they wore and the history those labels carried.

The names we use or are given to us can have powerful outcomes. In the same way, when we begin to investigate a local area, the stage on which people's lives have been played out, the meanings we associate with the names in that landscape are vital. The labels we pin on events, objects or people, and how we ourselves react to them, can have unexpected and sometimes serious consequences. This is equally true whether we are speaking of a time or place in the past, or categorising a person as 'well', 'ill' or 'foreign' today.

A map is a palimpsest[6] through time; a parchment on which layer upon layer of history has been written and over-written. Maps have four dimensions: the two-dimensional grid lines, altitude and, crucially, historical time. The story of the past on a map, as we reconstruct it from today, is the sum of the stories of the lives of the people who have passed their time in that place. And the names used of the past reflect and impact on our understanding of it.

Figure 1: An Approximate Time Line of Herefordshire from Prehistory to 1066

Prehistory	Neolithic (New Stone Age)	3,000 – 2,000 BC
	Bronze Age	2,000 – 800 BC
	Iron Age ('celtic', 'Welsh' or 'British')	after about 800 BC
Roman		47 – 410 AD
Early Medieval	sub-Roman	410 – 650
	Early Saxon	650 - 750
	Late Saxon (Mercian and English)	750 – 1066

We can see this clearly in the area around Studmarsh, the meadow on which Past in Mind was focussed. Poswick (in Whitbourne) – Possa's dairy farm; Tedstone – Teod's thorn-tree (a particularly beautiful tree? or was it a boundary marker?); Winslow – Wine's burial mound or meeting place.[7] All these people were Anglo-Saxon, and the place-names begin to reveal important facets of their lives and surroundings. We know nothing else about Possa in person, only his name, but we

---

6 see Glossary for definitions of technical terms
7 M Gelling, *The West Midlands in the Early Middle Ages*, ed. N Brooks (Studies in the Early History of Britain; Leicester: Leicester University Press, 1992), p. 52; D Hooke, 'Anglo-Saxon Landscapes of the West Midlands: The Charter Evidence' in *B.A.R. British* (1981); J Weale, *A History of Tedstone Delamere, in North-East Herefordshire* (Bromyard: Bromyard and District Local History Society, 2013), p. 4; P Williams, *Whitbourne, a Bishop's Manor* (Bromyard: Bromyard and District Local History Society, 1979), p. 88

know something of his daily life: a late-Saxon description of an estate manager's duties reveals that 'in August and September and October we mow, cut wood . . . thatch, cover over and clean out folds, make ready cow sheds and also pig-sties before too severe a winter come to the manor . . .'[8]

The story we have uncovered for Studmarsh goes far back into prehistory, just as our own lives can be shaped by early experiences. The names on the map begin in the pre-Roman, British, period. Most have been submerged in the flood of Anglo-Saxon culture that came later, but they cling on. Iron Age hill forts abound, including those nearby at Whitbourne[9], Grendon Bishop, Thornbury, Garmsley, Woodbury and Berrow, while further afield there are the great enclosures on the Malverns.[10] The names are indicative: -berrow and -bury derive in most instances from the Saxon word for a fortified place, revealing how they were perceived by these later settlers, who did not understand them. In fact, the 'hill forts' were probably seldom used in war; they were perhaps more a sign of prestige, to define territories, to demonstrate the authority of their rulers and to provide a social focus.

Figure 2: The parishes of the Studmarsh Area, with their Iron Age forts

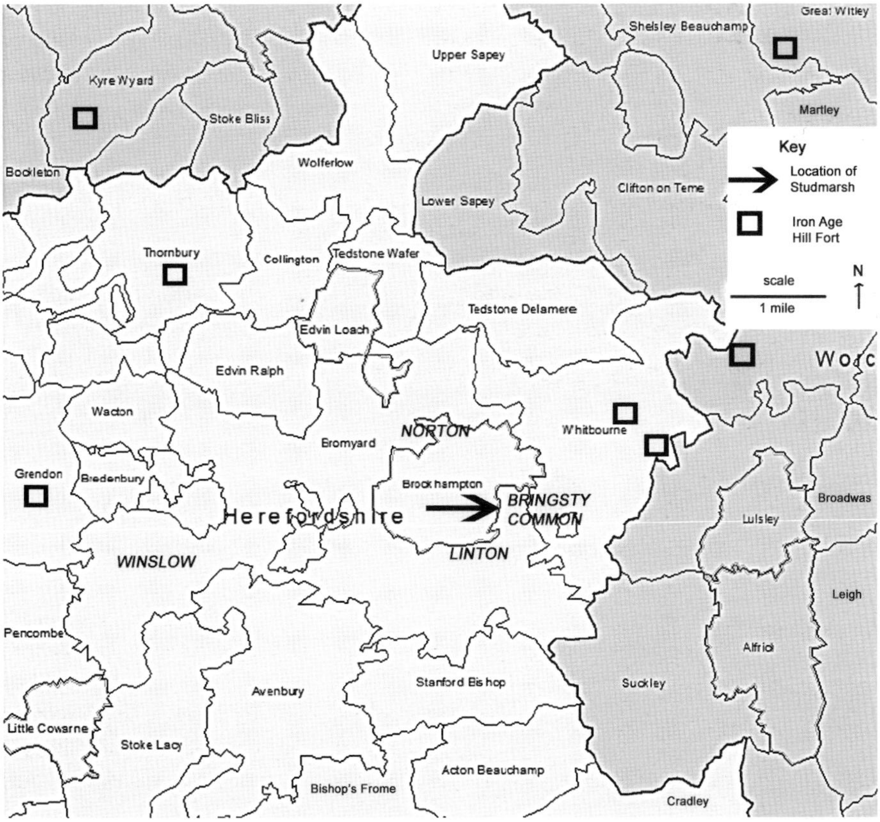

8 M Swanton, ed., *Anglo-Saxon Prose* (2nd edn; London: J.M.Dent, 1993)
9 see J Davies, 'Herefordshire', *Transactions of the Woolhope Naturalists' Field Club* 1900-1902 (1902): 248-84, p. 250, for a possible second small site north-west of Poswick Farm
10 G Children and G Nash, *A Guide to Prehistoric Sites in Herefordshire* (Monuments in the Landscape; Leominster: Logaston Press, 1994), pp. 90-95

There are other pre-Roman survivors on the map, so many that it is now thought that Herefordshire retained a significant British- (Welsh-) speaking population until at least the eighth century, long after the Saxon 'English' landed.[11] Pen- is a celtic word for a hill, and cwm (cumb, coomb) is a short more-or-less enclosed valley, so the nearby parish name of Pencombe is a pure British survivor. The river systems that define Studmarsh's landscape also retain their ancient names: Frome is the fair or brisk river, the Teme to the east is 'dark'. This tendency for river names to persist rather than be re-named by the Saxons is typical of a much wider phenomenon. Avon, Clun, Dart, Dee, Derwent, Exe, Severn, Tamar, Thames and Wye are all pre-English names. Why should this be? Were rivers so important for daily life that their names were tenaciously retained, or were they seen as mysterious, dangerous, to be placated or avoided? Certainly much of the surviving evidence suggests that they were named for their dark attributes, and people's tendency to make offerings at pools and rivers (which persists to this day in the urge to drop coins into fountains) has supplied archaeology with some of its most magnificent finds. Some rivers, including the Severn, were seen as so potent that the name (and perhaps the practice of placating it), was adopted by the Romans. Writing in about 115 AD, the Roman historian Tacitus called the river Sabrina, which probably derives from the name of the celtic river goddess worshipped upstream.[12] Perhaps the strange and sometimes terrifying Severn Bore played a part in setting the river apart from normal life.

Although no unambiguously pre-Roman discoveries were made at Studmarsh during our project, there is evidence for this phase of history in many other places in the locality. For example the suffix Bre- (as in Bredenbury), is another word for hill, in this case with an explanatory Old English –don, also meaning a hill. One of the families later associated with the Studmarsh land, the Combeys, may ultimately have derived their surname from the celtic cwm, meaning they were the people who lived in the little valley. From even earlier times, prehistoric tools and evidence for their manufacture also survive: scatters of flint are often found when land is ploughed, including a large number in Winslow, in Camp Field at Edvin Loach and on Bringsty Common.[13] Some beautifully crafted flint arrow heads, probably dating to the Bronze Age, have been found at Winslow, and most tantalising of all, a spindle whorl of unknown but probably pre-Roman date was found at the same site, giving a tiny keyhole view into the lives of long-past inhabitants, who obviously spun wool, and so kept sheep with all that this entails with stock management and control, as well as making and wearing woollen cloth.

Our understanding of what life was like at a particular period in the past, just like our comprehension of the lives of people in other places now, depends ultimately on the tools and techniques we use to study or analyse. What we see depends on how and where we decide to look, and even what it is that we want to find. The evidence for prehistoric life described above comes mainly from field walking and casual finds of material which does not easily decay. Another source of information, which can produce radically different, even conflicting evidence, is that which is

---

11 Gelling, *The West Midlands in the Early Middle Ages* , pp. 70-71
12 M Grant, ed., *Tacitus: The Annals of Imperial Rome* (Penguin Classics; London: Penguin, 2003), Book 12.31
13 Herefordshire Sites and Monuments Record, all within three miles of Studmarsh

now becoming available through the Portable Antiquities Scheme [PAS], because many of the finds brought to it are a result of systematic field walking linked to metal detecting. As a result, they may be biased to metal objects: coins, strap ends, buckles, swords and so on. Do these discriminate against the lives of those who had fewer metal objects, those people whose lives left a smaller 'footprint'? Do they skew the impression we form of different societies, which used metal goods for different purposes? We are accustomed to labelling people in certain ways, pigeon-holing them and drawing our conclusions; but we need to beware of judging societies of the past on the basis of our very imperfect knowledge about them. We know so little, and we can only see the tip of the iceberg, particularly for societies which have left no written records (plates 2 and 3).

Two PAS finds from near Studmarsh seem particularly significant. Another spindle whorl, of uncertain date but perhaps as early as the Neolithic, was found at Edvin Loach. Secondly, perhaps even more surprising, a golden Iron Age coin was discovered in Norton. On it is a stylised horse, similar to the one carved into the chalk at Uffington, Berkshire; below the horse a wheel is visible. Slightly further afield, four more Iron Age coins have been found, in Bishop's Frome, Leigh and Alfrick, and presumably others still await discovery. All four have images of horses and some also show the sun and moon, a wheel or a stylised tree. Intriguingly, one (dated to 120-60 BC) seems to have been a contemporary 'copy', since it is made of debased gold.[14] This use of horses on coins is perhaps an indication of their high status in pre-Roman culture, a status which continued well into the middle ages.

The Portable Antiquities database also includes some impressive Stone Age artefacts which add to the evidence for early human activity in the Studmarsh area.[15] Some of these finds are important in their own right, especially an axe head four inches long by two inches wide, made of hard-wearing igneous rock which has been carefully ground to produce a sharp blade. It has been dated to about 4000 BC, when such tools and the techniques for grinding them smooth were still new and rare.[16] Such a blade could have been an enormous asset when felling trees for timber, firewood or for agricultural clearance, as well as a status symbol. As a reminder that Neolithic people also killed animals, whether by hunting or selecting from farmed stock, there are also some beautiful arrow heads. They represent the changing styles of flint working, from 3500 to perhaps 1500 BC, with shapes ranging from triangular to a slender leaf form. And lest we doubt that these 'prehistoric' people were as intelligent as us, not witless savages, the occasional discoveries of finely-made flint scrapers and borers show that they knew a great deal about preparing skins and making leather garments. Of course, the level of sophistication of these communities is apparent as soon as we recall that there is no naturally-occurring flint or gold near Studmarsh, suggesting trading links with Wiltshire and south Wales, if not further. Although there is iron-ore in abundance in the Forest of Dean, it may not have been mined in pre-Roman times, so this

14 Early British coins were imported from Gaul or used Gallic (French) exemplars, and these in turn were ultimately copied from the gold coins of Philip of Macedonia, Alexander the Great's father, showing the king with his horse-drawn chariot. P Skingley, ed., *Coins of England and the United Kingdom* (41 edn; London: Spink and Son Ltd, 2006)
15 Based on a search of parishes in a six mile radius
16 Found in Cradley

too was perhaps traded over long distances in the Iron Age, with all the social complexities which this would involve.

The Roman period was the earliest for which the Studmarsh excavations produced firm evidence (plate 4). But it is worth pausing for a moment to think what we actually mean by this. By and large, the succession of prehistoric 'ages' – the Stone Ages, Bronze Age, Iron Age – are now understood to have developed from each other largely as a spread of new ideas, techniques and skills, rather than by conquest and invasion. Traders, innovators and some settlers certainly may have crossed the Channel, but it seems that the transition to, for example, agriculture in the Neolithic occurred primarily because of its benefits in assuring a more regular food supply, rather than as a result of a mass-invasion of Neolithic people. In other words, the name Neolithic does not strictly refer to a person, but to the situation and culture in which that person lived.

The Romans at first seem to be a very different category, since there was certainly a Roman invasion of Herefordshire in 47-77 AD, and significant numbers of troops, administrators and other 'Roman' people settled here. Studmarsh lies near the middle of a quadrilateral of important Roman towns: Worcester, a crossing-point of the River Severn and an iron-smelting centre; Droitwich (Salinae), a major salt-producer; Kenchester (Magnis), a regional administrative town; and Leintwardine, a large fort complex midway between the legionary fortresses of Chester and Caerleon. These four places epitomise the Roman conquest of Britain: roads and bridges, industrial activity, forts and soldiers, all associated with urban development.

Closer inspection, however, suggests that the Roman impact was somehow lighter. The structures changed, but did the people? We still use Roman roads, and many English and Welsh towns bear evidence of Roman planning, but about 90% of our 'Roman' place names are in fact linguistically British in origin; only a very few are purely Latin, and most of those are descriptive, such as Salinae, from the Latin for salt. This suggests that, while the administration was Roman, daily life continued much as before, using indigenous language and probably only slowly adopting new ways of living.[17] The problem is, of course, that without precise dating of find-types, the only things that can be definitely described as Roman are those which are different – imported, or made in new styles: the glossy red Samian ware pottery from Italy and southern Gaul, the classic 'villa' houses with mosaic floors. Yet even here the distinctions are not absolute, since by the middle of the Roman period, British potteries seem to have been competing successfully in the market for Samian-type pottery. Add all this to the relative scarcity of Latin loan-words in the English and Welsh languages, and a picture emerges of a Roman Herefordshire relatively unchanged from its Iron Age past, the rural population continuing to speak, farm and live much as they had done before the legionaries arrived. These people who at first seem so different, are quite 'normal' after all.

---

17 M Gelling, *Signposts to the Past: Place-Names and the History of England* (third edn; Chichester: Phillimore, 1997), pp. 32-39; A.L.F Rivet and C Smith, *The Place Names of Roman Britain* (London: Batsford, 1979)

Of the seven excavations carried out during the Studmarsh project, only one (Trench 1) produced finds which were dated to the Roman period. However, it must be remembered that neither of the main trenches (1 and 2) were fully excavated below the features dated as medieval, and three of the test pits (TP1, TP2 and TP3) were closed before their full potential was assessed.[18] The recent discovery of some very deeply buried Roman features in the county, and the much earlier chance find at Winslow of a probable Roman burial under four feet (*c.* 1.2m) of marl, are reminders that surface levels and deposits of clays in particular have in some instances changed markedly since the Roman era.[19] Do further Roman discoveries await us in Studmarsh?

The nine or ten pottery sherds from Studmarsh which were placed in the Roman period were all made locally, a mixture of the types known as Severn Valley ware and Malvernian ware. Some of these sherds could even date back into the pre-Roman, late Iron Age. All are likely have been made by 'native' potters, following Roman traditions and styles.[20] This seems to be typical of the Roman period in this area, although there are occasional local finds of imported pottery.

Local finds of Roman coins, however, tell a rather different story. Iron Age coins were high value and high status objects, unlikely to have been in regular use for trade but more probably made for rulers to exchange in order to cement alliances,[21] but the Roman imperial system depended on a supply of large numbers of low-denomination coins. Thus it is no surprise that over 20% of the 'Roman' objects recorded by the Portable Antiquities Scheme in the parishes near Studmarsh are coins. Three have been found in Whitbourne and another in Linton, on Bringsty Common, very near our site. As might be expected with coins in daily use, most are too worn to be identified securely, but two of these locally-discovered coins have been dated, to the reign of Titus in 79-81 AD (the earliest years of the Roman occupation of Herefordshire) and to Constans (346-350, almost at the end of the Roman era). These two particular coins were minted in Rome and Trier, Germany, respectively, giving an impression of the reach and complexity of Roman rule.[22]

There is also evidence nearby for the infrastructure of the occupation, with a Roman road running roughly north-south along the high ground to the north of Studmarsh, passing close to a small fort at Tedstone Wafer,[23] and another minor fort and road at Sapey Common. Other Roman-period buildings and roads have been found in nearby parishes, including Avenbury, Thornbury, Leigh and Knightwick.

So it seems that there was a sort of dual society operating during these centuries, with an official veneer of international Roman control, typified by the roads and

---

18 D Williams and C Atkinson, 'Studmarsh Medieval Settlement, Brockhampton, Herefordshire: A Summary Report on Excavations in August 2012' in *Herefordshire Archaeology Reports* (Hereford: Herefordshire Archaeology, 2013), pp. 27-29
19 Anon, 'Notes from the Winter Annual Meeting, 1932', *Transactions of the Woolhope Naturalists' Field Club* 1930-1932 (1935): xcix
20 S Ratkai, 'Pottery Report' in *Studmarsh Medieval Settlement, Brockhampton, Herefordshire*, ed. D Williams and C Atkinson (Hereford: Herefordshire Archaeology, 2012): 44-47
21 Skingley, ed., *Coins of England* , p. 2
22 WAW-748A66, silver denarius; WAW-1840D1, copper alloy nummus
23 G Webster, 'A Trial Trench across the Defences of the Roman Fort at Tedstone Wafer, Herefordshire', *Transactions of the Woolhope Naturalists' Field Club* 34 (1954): 284-87

forts that we associate with the Romans, but underlain by a largely unchanged celtic British society. It is the 'Roman' side of life that has left the footprint on history, and has determined the way those four centuries are viewed, because of the spectacular and more visible nature of the finds associated with it, but this only tells a small part of the story. Many more excavations of 'ordinary' sites, and more reports of chance finds of native-made pottery, are needed to help to redress the balance and tell the story of the Roman period though British eyes. As ever, it is the official story that is easier to read.

The Dark Ages?

If evidence and understanding are in short supply for rural Roman Herefordshire, they are almost wholly lacking for the period that followed, the time that is still often called The Dark Ages. There are several reasons for this. Firstly, whereas the kingdom of Wessex produced the Anglo-Saxon Chronicles, and Northumbria's history was written by the Venerable Bede (c. 731 AD), this part of England had no comparable chroniclers; or if it ever had, no trace survives. Secondly, Hereford was attacked and burnt during a Welsh raid in 1055, and many records and charters were probably destroyed, decimating another potential route into understanding this period. There are some surviving royal charters, but no wealth of detailed material comparable to that at Worcester, for example. Many of the charters that do survive are unfortunately of dubious reliability, because they were copied and collected at Llandaff in the twelfth century when Llandaff and Hereford dioceses were in dispute over their territorial claims; consequently, it is probable that the monks of Llandaff engaged in some creative editing. Thirdly, very few artefacts, whether pottery, jewellery or coins, have been dated to this period, so evidence for how people lived is very scarce. Indeed, the centuries from the end of the Roman era until shortly before the Norman conquest have been called 'aceramic' – a period with no pottery.

The Portable Antiquities finds seem to bear this out. Compared to the 85 Roman finds listed for the parishes around Studmarsh, there are only 4 for the whole early medieval period, which lasted nearly twice as long. None of these four finds were pottery: three are small copper-alloy strap fittings, while the fourth is a lead spindle whorl, decorated with what appear to be Anglo-Saxon runes; indeed, if it were not for this runic writing, the spindle whorl might have been dated to the Norman period, and we would have been left with only three.[24] The absence of coins can be readily explained. After Roman control collapsed, there was a period of about three hundred years when no coins seem to have been produced in this region, and trade was probably conducted by barter. Coins only began to be minted again in the reigns of Æthelbald (r. 716-757) and Offa (r. 757-796) of Mercia, and even then they were still relatively scarce. (Collectors today pay about ten times as much for Mercian and even later Anglo-Saxon coins as for Roman ones).[25] But it is much less easy to see how a society which had been manufacturing large

---

24 WMID-EA7BF5, found in Great Witley.
25 Skingley, ed., *Coins of England* ; S Zaluckyj, *Mercia: The Anglo-Saxon Kingdom of Central England* (2 edn; Leominster: Logaston Press, 2011), pp. 142-3, 160-162

quantities of pottery while the Romans were in power could have suddenly lost knowledge of the process, or the desire to use cooking pots and storage jars.

What does this label 'aceramic' mean? Does it really mean that there was no pottery in Herefordshire for about five centuries? Or did the population suddenly crash catastrophically, so there are few traces of human habitation left? Or is it in part a consequence of the habit of thinking of this period as the 'dark ages': a period of primitive survival, of uncivilised people disconnected from the Romans who went before and from the late-Saxon society of Alfred the Great and Edward the Confessor that ushered in the Normans? It is easier, perhaps, to think of such uncouth people not needing or wanting home comforts. But it is also plausible that (even allowing for a reduced use of pottery as fashions changed) sherds from this period could be being mis-identified, perhaps because they are so similar to so-called earlier or later types. Or insufficient 'dark age' sites may have been found and excavated for securely-datable evidence of their pottery to be obtained. At Hereford, an excavation into the early city walls found six phases of construction, and between two of these a group of 45 sherds were found, which were at first given a broad dating from 'Roman to fourteenth-century'. However their secure stratification helped with their later identification as 'Chester ware' cooking pots: the best dating evidence at the time came from a small hoard found in Chester in a vessel of this type, which included coins of about 970 AD, and the Hereford finds were consequently dated to *circa* 900-1050 AD.[26] At another major regional site, Wroxeter, most excavations have concentrated on the Roman city, which seems to have been abandoned by about 600 AD. By this time, a minster church probably existed on the site of the modern village, at the edge of the old city. Preliminary investigations at this 'dark age' religious site have found unusual pottery types which are provisionally dated to this post-Roman period.[27]

Without coinage and with the abandonment of many centres of population, it is hard to date post-Roman pottery.[28] Neither coins nor secure contexts are generally available in 'dark age' Herefordshire. Is this why the period with no coins appears to coincide with an 'aceramic' culture? There is a curious parallel here with the all-too-common assumption that people with mental ill-health are inherently unemployable. On the contrary, employment can yield crucial recovery results, but a precondition is the reversal of normally-applied yardsticks.

In three respects, the post-Roman centuries were indeed dark. There was a sudden deterioration of the climate, probably brought on in part by a major volcanic eruption and the subsequent dust cloud. A devastating outbreak of plague in 549 AD killed a large (although unquantified) proportion of the population. Lastly, and perhaps aided by the ravages of the plague among the native inhabitants, the pagan tribes who became known as the Anglo-Saxons moved west into Britain. Although this was not accompanied by wholesale slaughter as has sometimes

---

26 R Shoesmith, 'The Western Rampart', *Transactions of the Woolhope Naturalists' Field Club* 39 (1967): 51-67
27 P Barker, ed., (Worcester: West Mercian Archaeological Consultants Limited, 1990), especially Bassett and Moffett
28 A Vince, 'Did They Use Pottery in the Welsh Marches and the West Midlands between the Fifth and Twelfth Centuries A.D.?' in *From Roman Town to Norman Castle: Essays in Honour of Philip Barker*, ed. A Burl (Birmingham: Birmingham University Press, 1988): 40-55

been depicted, British leaders were certainly displaced amid war and social upheaval, significant numbers fled to Brittany and there is evidence that many native people became serfs or slaves. However, Anglo-Saxon culture probably spread by adoption as well as by conquest, and it was not until about 680 AD that it was established to the west of the River Severn.

Against this dark background is the undoubted fact that Herefordshire, and indeed much of Britain, was Christian through these so-called dark centuries. And because it was Christian, we know that at least some people were literate, since Christian communities need books. It must also have continued to been in contact with vine-growing and oil-producing lands, since church life requires wine and oil, and wine production in Britain was probably on the wane. Gildas, who in about 540 AD composed a commentary on contemporary events in this part of Britain from his base in south Wales, wrote in good Latin and clearly had access to a library containing a range of classical and early church texts.[29] As the Saxons spread out across England, they found many signs of Christian activity, some at least of which they respected and saved. This is seen most clearly in the place name Eccles and some of its compounds, derived as it is from the Latin ecclesia, for church. Places called Eccles from the Norfolk coast to Lancashire, from Kent to Dumfries and Galloway, bear witness to ancient religious centres, akin to modern cathedral cities or abbeys. One of these is in Herefordshire: Eccles Green, in Norton Canon parish, nine miles north-west of Hereford.[30] Another possible example is Eccleswall near Ross-on-Wye.[31]

By 700 AD, Saxon dioceses had been built upon these Romano-British foundations, centred in this region on Worcester and Hereford. Both of these were, co-incidentally, founded by men who formed a personal link with the old British churches, men who came from the Scottish borders and traced their conversion back to the celtic churches there. The existence of a bishopric means solid buildings, a literate staff of clergy, libraries and archives, journeys to Canterbury and even Rome, and regular contact with the outlying areas of the diocese. There may be few finds from this area which tell us about secular life in the early medieval period, but the evidence for its churches is there to see. Studmarsh was almost certainly part of a district administered and served from a mother church in Bromyard, which was founded at the latest by 840, from which time a surviving charter records a donation of land there. Several other nearby churches have evidence of Saxon stone-work, including Acton Beauchamp, Lower Sapey old church and Whitbourne, and there were other major churches at Leominster and Ledbury (plate 6).

So we can safely cease mis-naming this epoch as 'The Dark Ages', and instead call it Early Medieval, a vital period of nation-forming between the Roman and Norman eras.

29 M Winterbottom, ed., *Gildas: The Ruin of Britain, and Other Documents* (History from the Sources; Chichester: Phillimore and Co. Ltd., 1978)
30 Gelling, *The West Midlands in the Early Middle Ages* , p. 87
31 *Signposts to the Past* , pp. 98-101

Like the British who preceded them, and beside whom we must assume they settled and lived, the Saxons are not lost in their landscape, but very visible there when we look at the map. Most place names here are Saxon, and even without contemporary documents they are revealing. Bromyard (a thorn or broom enclosure), Brockhampton (a settlement by a stream), Bringsty (path along the bank edge or hill), Linton (place where flax was grown).[32] Some are descriptive of the landscape, while many are concerned with agriculture. The frequent use of –croft and –ley in place names, for small farmsteads in clearings, shows that the district remained more heavily wooded than the lands to the east, but it was certainly also being farmed, and many of its Saxon field systems and settlements are visible to this day.

Naming Studmarsh

The name Studmarsh itself is Saxon, but its meaning is not clear, which adds to the complexity of exploring its past. It is, if you like, a label we do not understand. The earliest known use of the name is in about 1285, perhaps 600 years after the site was first named by Germanic Saxon-speakers, so we have little idea of its history before this time. But by the late thirteenth century it was known variously as Stobmarshe, Stobmershe and Stubmarsh,[33] the first part of which is now thought to derive from stybb-, meaning a rooted-up tree or a tree stump. This suggests a clearance for agriculture, either by Saxon settlers or by their British predecessors or neighbours. The scarcity of this name element hints that the process of clearance or the appearance of this piece of land might have been significant in some way; perhaps it was unusually hard to clear, or the tree stumps were still conspicuous? The earlier proposal for a meaning of 'land where horses are kept' is less likely for etymological reasons, and is implausible if the meadow was also wet: in Saxon society as before and since, horses were high-status animals, and they do not cope well with marsh-land. The second name element could mean 'boundary land' or 'marshy land' or even, possibly, 'land of the Mercians': people from further north, rather than members of the local (Magonsætan) grouping of Saxons.[34] These possibilities will need further exploration later on.

Perhaps symbolically, the two families which we discovered were most closely associated with the history of Studmarsh both had surnames originating in the Saxon period. Colley is a name particularly associated with the West Midlands, from an Old English word for dark or swarthy. Did it perhaps begin as a nickname for a person with Welsh (British) blood compared with the predominantly fair Saxons? If so, it might not be stretching the case too much to suggest it was an unflattering description, even a pejorative term. The other family name, Biddle (alias Beedle, Bidel etc.) on the other hand derives from the Old English bydel, Middle English bedele, an occupational name for a junior court official. Nine places

32 B Coplestone-Crow, *Herefordshire Place Names* (2 edn; Leominster: Logaston Press, 2009)
33 The Red Book, Hereford; BDLHS AW.B56/1/37-45
34 Coplestone-Crow, *Herefordshire Place Names* , p. 58; Hooke, 'Anglo-Saxon Landscapes of the West Midlands: The Charter Evidence' , p. 175; P Williams, *Bromyard: Minster, Manor and Town* (Bromyard: Bromyard and District Local History Society, 1987), p. 72

in the Herefordshire section of Domesday Book are listed as having a beadle.[35] By Shakespeare's time it was used for a village constable.[36] At some point, these monikers must have become attached to particular people, and by the fifteenth century they would have been in regular use as surnames, inherited through the male line on marriage.

And Finally . . .

Studmarsh has also been named in a different way. Before this project began, it had been described as a 'Deserted Medieval Village' on the Herefordshire SMR. As the archaeological report notes, however, the label Deserted is not strictly accurate, since the adjacent buildings at The Grove are still occupied; indeed, into the twentieth century the building flanking the site on the east was also inhabited. Shrunken is a more accurate term than deserted.[37] This name Deserted Medieval Village, however commonly used it has been, has other consequences: like any of the names we have been considering, it can pigeon-hole and confine in unhelpful ways. It may not seem to matter too much whether Studmarsh is referred to as a village or a settlement, except to specialists, but the two words give a very different impression of what it would have been like to live there: a large thriving community, or a small isolated cluster of houses. Calling it medieval is even more perilous: there is a danger that the whole history we have explored so far, and much of that which comes after the 'medieval' times, will be overlooked or given insufficient weight. There is also, surely, a risk that if we go looking for medieval settlements, then that is all that we will see. Mis-naming things causes misconceptions, and the labels and consequences can stick.

This problem should also alert us to the different approaches taken by the various disciplines involved in the uncovering of the past, to the ways in which they can contribute to a shared understanding as well as to the tensions between them. Different disciplines use their own vocabulary, and focus on different aspects of a problem. We need to be aware of the advantages but also the pitfalls of interdisciplinary work before we can benefit from it. This is all part of a separate and broader issue, to which we now need to give some thought: namely the consequences of life on the margins.

---

35 C.W Atkin, 'Herefordshire' in *The Domesday Geography of Midland England*, ed. H.C Darby and I.B Terrett (2 edn; Cambridge: Cambridge University Press, 1971): 57-114, p. 71

36 P Hanks et al., ed., *The Oxford Names Companion: The Definitive Guide to Surnames, First Names and Place Names of the British Isles* (Oxford: Oxford University Press, 2002)

37 Williams and Atkinson, 'Studmarsh Medieval Settlement' , p. 9

Chapter 3. On the Margins

The Past in Mind project sits on and is defined by margins. It is based on a new and therefore marginal methodology, a cross-fertilization between the recovery model in mental health and a community heritage project. The recovery model offers a personal identity beyond the label of 'mental health patient', builds on existing skills and aspires to empower individuals across boundaries, just as local heritage work empowers and trains participants. At the same time, Past in Mind is an extreme example of inter-disciplinary study, a way of working which is fashionable but fraught with danger, increased in this case because there are not two but three or four different disciplines involved. And in the course of the research, a whole range of internal margins were uncovered, each contributing to the understanding of the site and its story through human history.

We have already seen how a map can be read carefully to reveal the way a landscape has been repeatedly modified through time by succeeding generations, and is something which can be interpreted by understanding the history it reveals. Similarly, a medieval document has greater value for the modern reader if it has 'marginalia' – comments, annotations, diagrams, even scribbles, from its readers. Such a document not only tells us what the original writer wanted to say, or what he was supposed to be copying; it also sheds light on the lives of the people who have read the text at different times. From monks complaining of cold fingers while creating the manuscript, to scurrilous sketches added by readers years later, all comments in the margins supply added layers of meaning, more dimensions, a more complex palate, through the interventions of more people through time. Without space in the margins, this material would not be available.

In the same way, a research project which sets out to push the boundaries (that word again!) of what is achievable in terms of the number of different viewpoints and disciplines it involves, may be more difficult but it also offers more opportunities. There will be opportunities for discoveries, for shared understanding, for appreciating the limits of one's own knowledge and expertise, and for new ways of learning. Despite its limitations, this is above all what the Past in Mind project has demonstrated.

Studmarsh: A Place on the Margins

Mental ill-health marginalises people, regardless of their actual human potential. Correspondingly, we have found that the little piece of land at Studmarsh has been marginal in a whole variety of ways, for much of its known history. Even today eastern Herefordshire, where it sits, is hard to define. It is marginal country, neither urban West Midlands nor Welsh Borders, neither North nor South West. Being deeply rural, it tends to pass under the radar of the great and good, and it was no surprise to many Herefordshire people when a certain Westminster politician seemed confused between it and Hertfordshire. There are more, and more visible, people in Hertfordshire!

As far back as we can go into recorded history, this landscape has been marginal, beginning with the boundaries between three ancient British tribes who were encountered by the Romans: the Silures, Dobunnii and Cornovii. The Silures' lands extended from Herefordshire across Brecon and into south Wales; the Dobunnii's power base ran east and south into Wiltshire; the Cornovii were centred on Shropshire. So at times, Studmarsh could have been at the uneasy meeting point of all three of these tribal groups. Of course, we know almost nothing about these people except in terms of what the Romans tell us: we only see them as outsiders saw them.

For a short while, Herefordshire was the Roman frontier as the occupation moved west. But south Wales soon came under Roman control, and for much of the Roman period Studmarsh would have been well within the settled landscape, an unusual period away from the margins.

In post-Roman times, as we have seen, things were not quite as dark as they have been painted. For two centuries and more, the 'native' British people here were largely untroubled by the advancing Germanic peoples we call the Anglo-Saxons. Unlike mainland Europe, where Christianity and hence 'civilisation' remained based in towns and cities, life in Britain seems to have become more rural, centred on country estates and small religious shrines. The Book of Llandaff, assembled in the twelfth century, names nearly 80 monasteries (many of them with only a handful of monks) and churches spread over south Herefordshire and south-east Wales in the immediate post-Roman period. The evidence on the ground gives some credence to this otherwise rather dubious source.

Studmarsh sat at the edge of what must have been a significant British diocese, probably associated with the kingdom of Ergyng, later known as Archenfield, and founded by St Dyfrig (c. 450-540 AD). Although not widely remembered today, Dyfrig (or Dubricius, to use his Latinised name) was a major figure in early medieval British history, one who deserves greater respect. He founded many important monastic schools, and taught several of Ergyng's early leaders and teachers, a century before St Augustine arrived at Canterbury. At the peak of its power and territorial extent, Ergyng may have reached from the Malverns to the Black Mountains and from the Severn to the Wye above the Dore Valley. Evidence for this period in the history of Herefordshire survives in church dedications to Dyfrig and other founding fathers, and in early place names like Hentland (a British name meaning 'the old church'). There are also some stone carvings which may date back as far as the pre-Saxon period, such as those at Upton Bishop, Llangarron and Linton by Ross (plate 7). There is much less information available about the lands further to the north, but we do know that when Augustine reached Kent in 597 AD, and proposed a meeting with the British bishops, they gathered to discuss the idea at a major monastery called Bangor-is-Coed, near Wrexham.[38] Even the Saxon Bede, with his anti-British bias, concedes that this monastery was very large.

---

38 J McClure and R Collins, ed., *Bede: The Ecclesiastical History of the English People, the Greater Chronicle and Bede's Letter to Egbert* (Oxford: Oxford University Press, 1969), book II.2

Plate 1. Studmarsh Meadow: aerial view from the north-east. The Grove farm is at the top, towards the right hand corner, and the hedge marking the northern limit of the site runs from there down to the trees of Bond's Dingle. At the left hand edge, the enclosures of the ruined cottage and its garden can be seen, on the edge of the common. (J. K. St Joseph, 1956)

Plate 2. Top. In the meadow: an introduction to surveying. (Past in Mind archive)
Bottom. A spindle-whorl, perhaps dating to the Neolithic, found near Studmarsh at
Edvin Loach. (Portable Antiquities Scheme)

Plate 3. Top. Arrow head, perhaps dating to the Bronze Age, found at Hanley William, six miles from Studmarsh. Bottom. Golden Iron Age quarter stater coin, found at Leigh. (Portable Antiquities Scheme)

Plate 4. Three sherds of Roman-era pottery found in Trench 1 during the Studmarsh excavation. Top: Severn Valley ware; middle: Malvernian ware; bottom: coarser Malvernian ware perhaps from a large storage jar.

Plate 5. Top. Examples of Severn Valley ware vessel types. (© Worcestershire Archive and Archaeology Service) Bottom. Project members excavating Trench 1. (Past in Mind archive)

Plate 6. Top. Part of a Saxon cross re-used as a lintel at Acton Beauchamp church. Bottom. Carving of St Peter, probably Saxon in date, set into a later wall at Bromyard church.

Plate 7. Examples of carvings from near Ross on Wye which probably date to the pre-Saxon Kingdom of Ergyng. Top: Upton Bishop; bottom left: Llangarron (thought to be a Christian priest); bottom right: cross at Linton-by-Ross.

Plate 8. A wood-cutting scene from a late-Saxon calendar of the Labours of the Months, with two draught oxen and a detailed drawing of a farm cart. As the population expanded, more wood was needed for fuel and building, and additional land was cleared for growing crops. The name Studmarsh is probably derived in part from the stumps remaining after its trees were felled. (© The British Library Board, Cotton Tiberius B.V, Part 1, f.6)

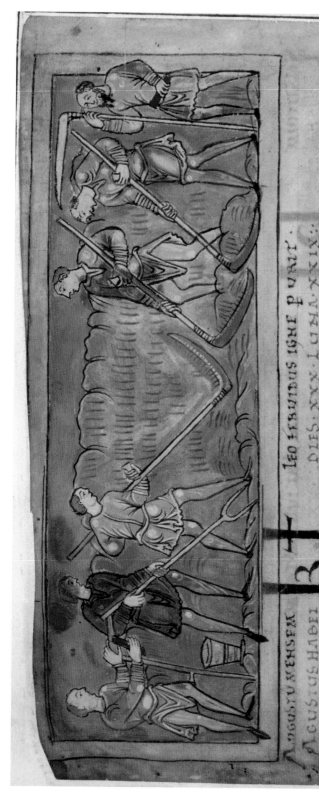

Plate 9. Harvest was a community project in the middle ages. Using scythes or sickles, and sharpening them on the job, men worked through the daylight hours to bring in the staff of life which was used for making bread, ale and soup. Beginning the harvest in July, they aimed to have the first loaves baked with the new grain in time for Lammas, the feast of 'loaf mass' on 1st August. (© The British Library Board, Cotton Tiberius B.V, Part 1, f.6v)

Plate 10. Top. Trees and timber were a significant theme in the Studmarsh fieldwork. A pedunculate oak tree estimated to be about 450 years old, growing near the house excavated in Trench 1, suggested an end-point for its occupation, while felled trees in the meadow provided a convenient lunch-base. (Past in Mind archive) Bottom. This model gives an impression of rural life in early-medieval Britain, with wooden buildings, predominantly arable crops and an enclosure around the settlement.

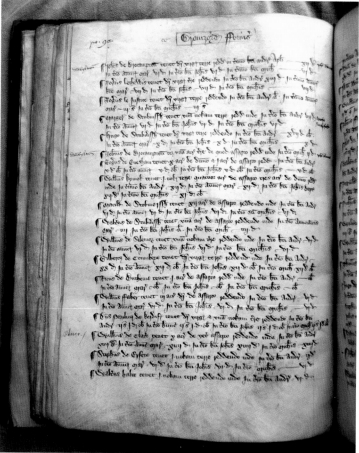

Plate 11. Top. *The Red Book* of the bishop of Hereford, *circa* 1285. Bottom. This page of *The Red Book* lists some of the bishop's free tenants in Linton and Norton. They include John of Brockhampton (lines 1-2), Margaret and Hugh of Studmarsh (lines 7 -10), the assarts of Matilda and Walter of Studmarsh (17 -20) and Gilbert of Coumbeye's land (23-24).

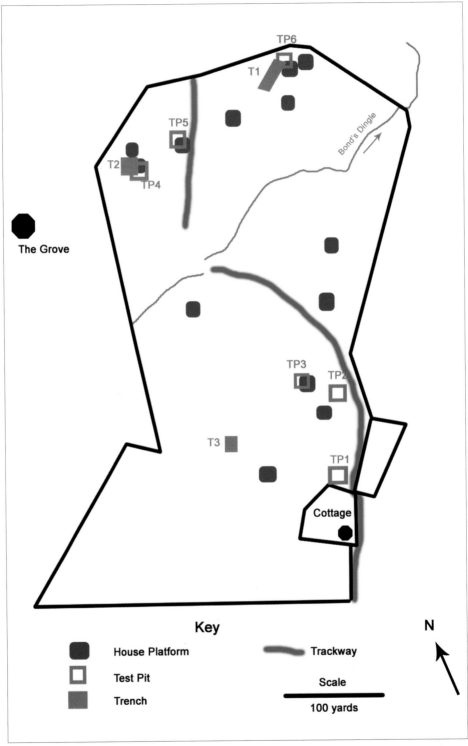

TP6

T1

TP5

Bond's Dingle

T2

TP4

The Grove

TP3

TP2

T3

TP1

Cottage

Key

House Platform

Trackway

Test Pit

Scale

Trench

100 yards

N

Plate 12. Sketch map of the site showing the tracks and platforms which have been identified, and the locations of the test pits and trenches which were excavated.

Plate 13. The early stages of any exploration into the past are about learning new techniques. Top: recording the survey results; middle: sieving and looking for 'finds' (both pictures, Past in Mind archive); bottom: digging down systematically through the layers. (Dai Jones)

Plate 14. Medieval pottery sherds found at Studmarsh, pre-dating the plagues and famines; fabric type B1. Top: pot rim dating to the early fourteenth century (T1 016); middle: fragment with residual surface detail, twelfth- to early fourteenth-century (TP3 003); bottom: late thirteenth-century rim (T1 unstratified).

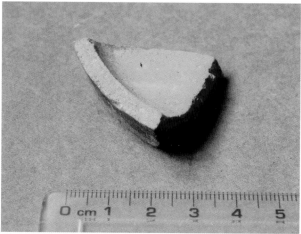

Plate 15. Top and middle: exterior and interior views of a fragment of the base of a B4 fabric late-medieval cooking pot (T1 008); bottom: a display of medieval pottery at the Hereford Museum Resource and Learning Centre.

Plate 16. Top: uncovering the evidence in Trench 2; middle and bottom: the house in Trench 1. (Dai Jones)

Figure 3: The Maximum Extent of the Kingdom of Ergyng

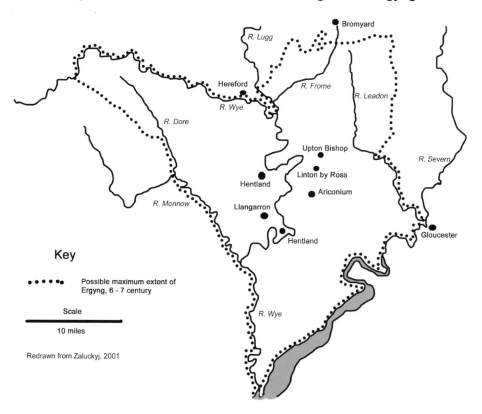

Key

● ● ● ● ●● Possible maximum extent of
Ergyng, 6 - 7 century

Scale

10 miles

Redrawn from Zaluckyj, 2001

Soon after Dyfrig's death, the Anglo-Saxons won an important battle at Dyrham, in Somerset, and this led to the temporary invasion of much of Herefordshire. The Book of Llandaff says that for a while 'the heathen Saxon race' caused 'great tribulations' here, and after they were repulsed and the land returned to its former owners, much of it was found to be laid waste 'with men few and far between'.[39] Nor did things return to their former state for long. Instead, Archenfield passed at first under the control of the king of Gwent, and then later to a tribe of Anglo-Saxon in-comers. The sequence of events is not understood, and probably never will be because there is so little documentary evidence. But we can assume that the Studmarsh area remained 'on the margins', with the pagan Saxon king Penda, who now ruled the area to the north (perhaps centred on Lichfield) making an uneasy alliance with the Christian Welsh in his battles against the Saxon kings of Northumbria. It may be that this alliance paved the way for a relatively peaceful take-over of the Herefordshire part of Archenfield and its incorporation into the Anglo-Saxon orbit.

Although the modern boundaries of Herefordshire may have been emerging at this time, it was not immediately joined to Mercia, the Saxon kingdom created by Penda. Instead, a separate and quite small unit was formed, called the

39 S Baring-Gould and J Fisher, ed., *The Lives of the British Saints* (2 edn; Felinfach: Llanerch Facsimile Reprints, 2000), volume 4, p. 362

Magonsæte, and this probably survived for two generations of rulers. So for a century or more, Studmarsh was probably in a very marginal place indeed. To the north, it was painfully close, perhaps just a few miles, to the border between the growing power of the Mercian kingdom which later dominated most of Anglo-Saxon England, and the smaller kingdom of the Magonsæte which was soon to be engulfed by Mercia. Culturally, Studmarsh was still part of an old Christian civilisation, but surrounded by an in-coming tide of rulers and settlers only very recently converted from their paganism, and with strange and unfamiliar ways. And socially it was a borderland place, where these two cultures would continue to co-exist, speaking their two different languages, for some time to come, maybe as late as 900 AD, the time of Alfred the Great and the Viking invasions, or perhaps even up to the Norman Conquest.

This marginal location continues up until today. The county and diocesan boundaries are barely five miles to the north and east. Studmarsh sits hard by the boundary between the two parishes of Whitbourne and Bromyard, while the township boundary between Linton and Norton runs through the middle of the meadow itself. The antiquity of this boundary is suggested by the existence of the hollow way along part of its length, a feature which hints that the route may have been recognised and used for many years. Moreover, Studmarsh is on the very edge of the farmed land, next to the 'common waste' of Bringsty Common. Commons may have been unploughed in medieval agriculture, but they were by no means useless. Villagers had rights to collect wood, feed pigs, graze stock at certain times of year, harvest wild fruits, and a duty to guard their commons against abuse, especially by outsiders. Studmarsh was at the junction of the arable or pasture farmed lands and these common resources, and judging by its name it had also been cleared of its own trees (and so perhaps withdrawn from

Figure 4: The Site Area, on the Linton, Norton and Whitbourne boundaries

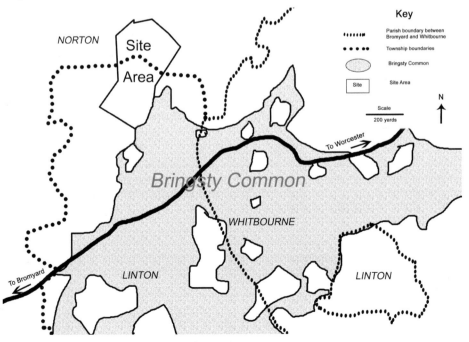

the commons) relatively recently when it came under Anglo-Saxon control. This fundamental fact of its location may explain the other part of its name, -mershe, a border or boundary land, which comes into modern English in the 'Welsh Marches'.

How ancient are these parish and township boundaries? There is no certain and robust proof in an area like Herefordshire, with very poor survival of Saxon boundary charters, but we do have one remarkable regional clue, based on Offa's dyke. It has been observed that parish boundaries seldom cross major Roman roads (which long preceded them), but end at the roadsides as if they were an acknowledged and visible mark in the landscape; railways by contrast usually cut across parishes and even individual fields. In the same way, it can be shown that the great majority (about 80%) of parish boundaries along Offa's dyke do not respect it, but instead are cut in half by it, and moreover several of the boundaries that do follow the dyke are demonstrably later sub-divisions of large parishes. This suggests, astonishingly, that the majority of the land along the Welsh Marches, and so presumably that further east as well, was already 'settled' in the sense of being divided up by accepted boundaries for exploitation as farms, parishes and estates, by the reign of King Offa (757-796 AD) at the very latest.[40] An obvious conclusion to draw, in the absence of firmer evidence, would be that the boundaries around Studmarsh, the margins on which it sits, had already been laid down by the Saxon period, some thirteen hundred years ago. Even though Studmarsh is marginal and apparently unimportant, it carries a very ancient heritage.

In the same way as we began this section by noting the importance and value of comments written in the margins of manuscripts, so we can end by observing that marginal sites like Studmarsh are vitally important for understanding the health and prosperity of rural populations and indeed nations through time. Long periods of relative peace and freedom from famine, such as much of England experienced in the two centuries after the Norman Conquest, certainly led to the margins being pushed back; to new land being brought under the plough; to less suitable (more marginal) land being farmed, often at the expense of woodland; and to a rising population. Conversely, disastrous years like the wet decade in the early 1300s, especially when followed by a calamity such as the Black Death and the other plagues which followed it, led to a withdrawal from the margins which is still visible in the landscape today, in abandoned arable fields in areas since covered by what we tend to think of as 'ancient' woodland. At times like these, life became more marginal while the margins of the intensively used land shrank back. In good times, the boundaries are pushed, while in bad times, there is a retreat from the margins.

It would be wrong, however, to assume that the wider ways in which Studmarsh was marginal made it inherently more prone to shrinkage or abandonment. In medieval England, with high transport costs and poor information flow, each small area of the nation, each parish or township, had to be correspondingly more self-sufficient. People still strove to feed themselves from their own resources, and the margins would only move when absolutely necessary. Studmarsh is not marginal in the sense of being infertile or mountainous, merely that it lies on margins

---

40 Bapty, I. *pers comm.*; M Gelling, *The West Midlands in the Early Middle Ages*, ed. N Brooks (Studies in the Early History of Britain; Leicester: Leicester University Press, 1992), pp. 104-5

defined by cultural forces. In the early middle ages, its marginality was defined by its position on geopolitical boundaries, but with few exceptions that had ceased to be the case by the 1300s. The definition of the marginal, in other words, is constantly changing as external factors alter.[41]

People and a Project on the Margins

The Past in Mind project as a whole was marginal in the sense of being radically inter-disciplinary. This is of course both an opportunity and a danger. Margaret Gelling has highlighted the perils awaiting the historian or archaeologist who tries their hand at place-name studies, noting that 'it is a commonplace of Dark Age studies that philologists, historians and archaeologists do not always appreciate each other's points of view'. Words like catastrophic and disaster-prone seem harsh, but Gelling is probably realistic in using them to warn against unwary forays into another person's specialism.[42] With three main disciplines, Archaeology, Social History and Mental Health Recovery collaborating on this project, it was inevitable that some blunders occurred, and it is a source of great satisfaction that there were not more. The project showed up the dangers of interdisciplinary work, especially within a tight budget and a short time-frame, but it was also about discovering the creative opportunities such work can bring. Like the marginal annotations on an ancient document, this place of interface can be a rewarding and productive area for study.

Having mental health recovery models at its heart was obviously the most radical and exciting part of the project, and offered many opportunities for exploring life at the margins. Mental health recovery can be seen as the ownership of a process of careful learning and uncovering of layers of meaning – a perfect analogy for the historical and archaeological elements of the project. Whether we are thinking of the archaeological, historical or mental health domains, real progress and genuinely creative work can only occur within a structured framework.

At the same time, it is true that those experiencing mental health problems can feel they are 'living on the margins' where they are somehow out of touch and so have few opportunities to make a valid or valued contribution to the culture in which they have to live. Can a marginal place like Studmarsh can be seen as a model for these under-valued lives? Perhaps significantly, only the 'insiders' of medieval England (the literate, the monastic) were able to contribute marginalia for the documentation of their times. The Past in Mind project pushed hard at the boundaries of what can be achieved, but actually all three of its core disciplines share a marginal place in modern British society. We know only too well that funding for health services and especially for mental health is under severe pressure, but this is something which all the project disciplines have in common. Most archaeology and history projects also find funding hard to come by. Yet like mental health care, a society which has no appreciation of or concern for its

---

41 M Bailey, 'The Concept of the Margin in the Medieval English Economy', *The Economic History Review* New Series 42 (1989): 1-17

42 M Gelling, *Signposts to the Past: Place-Names and the History of England* (third edn; Chichester: Phillimore, 1997), p. 1

historical roots, and does not value this dimension of its life, is in danger of being adrift and directionless. Similarly, the many marginalised people in modern rural communities are frequently left floundering, because 'poverty comes thatched here' and so it often goes unremarked while more visible and 'conventional' urban problems attract attention.

There may be a further parallel, with the experience of the Mercians themselves: a mysterious people about whose origins we know so little but who had a clear sense of who they were, defining themselves as Mierce – the people on the boundary. We do not even know which boundary they were so aware of. Did they feel they were on the edge of the more powerful Anglo-Saxon kingdom of Northumbria to their north-east? Or were they uncomfortably positioned at the very edge of the Germanic settlements, next to the celtic folk in Wales? These boundary-dwellers are often defined as who they were not, and so the Mercians' successful conquests far to the east until London was briefly their main port seem improbable for such a shadowy people.

Past in Mind worked at the boundaries in other important ways. In common with other community heritage projects, of which there have now been several in Herefordshire, it worked with a mix of professionals and amateurs. This situation was further complicated since some of the professionals were working largely as volunteers, because of funding constraints, while others were paid for their segment of the work. The amateurs were themselves made up of 'experts' and 'beginners'; some were Mind service users, others were drawn from the local community. Crucially, however, all these amateurs remained in an undifferentiated group, and it was a fundamental principle of the project that no attempt was made to distinguish between them. No-one was separated off or categorised, except perhaps in their reaction to the bull who took an excessive interest in some of the field work! The team, in other words, was designed from the outset to have no internal divisions, no boundaries, and no margins. As a result, some of the barriers raised by preconception and prejudice were reduced during the project. This was a risk, but as discussed in Chapter 1, it was fundamental to the project design from the start. Some of the barriers which emerged were unexpected, such as a hostility to or fear of 'history' because of deep-seated associations with its political and cultural overtones. All these preconceptions had to be respected and worked with. Other participants discovered hidden assumptions, both in themselves and sometimes in others, relating to mental health problems, which were gradually modified.

It was always envisaged that the project, especially its archaeological component, would have a synergistic, mutually enhancing interaction with mental health recovery. For some participants that was a fiercely challenging process, whether they were newcomers to an understanding of mental health, illness and well-being, or whether they were already Mind service users. For many, the project provoked dramatic and roller-coaster change. Few remained untouched in some way, and new friendships and connections were made as participants discovered new potentials and interests.

A spin-off from this blending of academic and amateur was that the public presentation of the project results was freed up to challenge conventional notions of what outcomes and interpretations of history are 'acceptable'. This flowed into the perpetual debate about the acceptability of historical drama as an expression of truth. In the stage enactment of 'A Day in the Life' (Chapter 7), feelings and imagined situations were given as much space as 'fact', and it was the more creative interpretations which were felt to have got closer to the spirit of the ages they represented. This in turn relates closely to the core value of ownership of the recovery process.

The project worked at the three-way boundary between past lives, the past of contemporary lives and present living. Several of the amateurs involved in the archaeological dig commented on the strong sense of a bond between themselves and the people whose houses, broken pots and grassland they were handling. This is a common but under-acknowledged experience in much historical work, and it may be one of the main reasons why people are attracted to archaeology. Bridging the gap of centuries is a potent, almost tangible, discovery.

The margins are, as we have seen, important and creative places if they are handled sensitively. Tribal and estate boundaries would have needed to be fixed when population pressure reached the point where there was no more 'spare' land into which to spread. This may have occurred as early as pre-Roman times, and the evidence suggests that it was achieved in the Studmarsh area by the 700s at the latest. Once boundaries are fixed, meeting points are needed for those from tribal sub-divisions, and for those who come to trade from 'other' peoples. To the east, we have the example of Knightwick, five miles from Studmarsh where the main road crosses the River Teme. Knightwick probably derives its name from 'the men of the Hwicce', the neighbouring kingdom which equated to modern Worcestershire. This, then, was a barrier on a boundary, a place defined by difference, maybe a warning of where you should not go without permission. Conversely, perhaps, the parish boundary on Bringsty Common would have represented security for Studmarsh people, and an assertion of rights not available to those from elsewhere. These concepts feed into the debate on security versus freedom. We see it in arguments over institutionalised living versus care and residence in the community, and equally in political and social arguments about the porosity of national borders. Do barriers make people feel safe, and if so is this for the people inside or outside? Who defines barriers? Who pays for them? Once built, do they become self-fulfilling or can they be modified without undue pain? If we relate this to internal personal barriers, whether they are the safety mechanisms of the chronically shy or the coping strategies of those with episodic mental illness, the pay-off between social engagement and feelings of security can seem both a blessing and a curse for those 'on the other side' of a boundary.

Herefordshire is an unusual county in so many ways. The Anglo-Saxons arrived here so late, and settled so slowly, that archaeologically it is unlikely to yield any dramatic pagan finds like the ship burial of Sutton Hoo. This must also have had important social consequences. Far from the British 'surviving', clinging on in a predominantly Anglo-Saxon culture, much of Herefordshire probably remained predominantly British-speaking until nearly the time of the Norman Conquest;

even in the extreme north of the county Saxon culture only took over from the tenth century. This radically alters the story of these centuries. What was it like to live here during these times of change, either for the Saxons in the early years when few of their neighbours would have understood them or looked kindly on them, or at the time of the Conquest, when the British had lost their identity in one cultural transition, only to find their land taken over by new rulers, speaking in another unfamiliar language? And what of the first Norman settlers; did they, too, feel isolated and vulnerable?

Chapter 4. People in the Landscape

Studmarsh today is a meadow. As you first see it, it is a high piece of ground to the north, a small valley and then a long slope rising gently up to the main road east out of Bromyard, the road to Worcester and ultimately to London. It is quickly driven by, and easily missed until you know it. It is only closer contact that reveals the steepness of the northern ridge, subtle changes in the soils, the rather more obvious variations in drainage.

The meaning you place on a landscape depends on how you look at it. It is culturally, socially and sometimes emotionally loaded, because its interpretation varies according to who and where you are. For an early-medieval farming community, life must have been largely defined by the cycle of the seasons in a small locality: perhaps a five mile radius of 'home'. Into this might come traders from distant places, but to return with them was seldom an option. The landscape was limited by the surrounding hills and streams, its quality determined by soil and vegetation. For those of servile status, tied to the land, the horizons were closer and life still further constrained by the weather and the produce of personal labour. Even for the early-modern villagers of the seventeenth and eighteenth centuries, leaving your parish of birth was not a safe option unless there was a guarantee of work at your destination, be it a known or unknown place. Whatever the constraints, however, these 'people of the land' still had opportunities to shape their landscape and lives, in small but important ways: to mend fences, fertilize fields and plough straight furrows. And some did move to 'pastures new'. For the rich, the mobile and the free, by contrast, landscape has a very different meaning. It is a source of wealth, a place for leisure, a broad expanse with wide physical bounds. A place you can pass by without much thought.

We can begin to put names to the people in the Studmarsh landscape, to identify them as individuals, from about a thousand years ago, and even before this we can name some of their neighbours. We also have keyhole glimpses of their lives, through contemporary documents and the illustrations of the agricultural 'labours of the months' (plates 8 and 9). We can surmise that this basic way of life was the norm through much of the long period of cultural transition between the Romans and the late Saxon period. In these centuries with few coins and with little other certain dating evidence, we simply do not know where or how most people in Herefordshire spent their lives. They seem to have lived in timber houses, in small and scattered settlements, with a predominantly barter economy, while those items of pottery which were used may have been similar to those that had been locally made for years. If the structures uncovered in our Trench 2 were indeed domestic, their modest size, lack of artefacts and their wattle and daub construction might be typical of most homes for many generations.

We do know that the weather began to improve after the cool, damp years of the sixth century, so that by about 1000 AD the summers were warm and dry, in the so-called Medieval Warm Period. This encouraged a change from growing barley to the much pleasanter bread-wheat, which flourished in the better conditions. Two of the last poor harvests of the bad old years may be those bewailed in the

Anglo-Saxon Chronicles for 1042 and 1044, for their low yields and high wheat prices. Despite the severe hardship of such years, these chronicle entries do suggest that coinage was circulating more freely and markets were functioning as distribution points in a recognisable economy. The transfer to wheat, pleasant as it was, was not an unmixed blessing. When the weather deteriorated again in the latter part of the thirteenth century, the wheat crops were unable to ripen as barley or rye might have done. The landscape and the fields of home, which had been a relatively safe and generous place, became unfriendly; famine returned and by the early 1300s starvation was a commonplace after bad harvests.

Apart from hazy references to settlements of monks in southern and western Herefordshire, the earliest names we know are of the ruling classes. Indeed, many priests and bishops like Dyfrig were themselves of royal blood. These were the minority who were not constrained by the local landscape, whose relationship with it was not so confined, people who as a result of their wider and freer horizons may have missed the detail that others felt.

So, for example, we know that sometime between 704 and 709 AD, Bishop Tyrhtil of Hereford granted several hundred acres of his land at Fulham to the bishop of London. This is not only very early evidence for a bishopric at Hereford, but it shows that Tyrhtil had contacts across the whole of southern England. For him and for others of his high status, life was wider than Herefordshire, and we can imagine him making journeys, perhaps regularly and with a sizeable entourage, to London and elsewhere.[43]

The first person who comes into any sort of focus in the landscape near Studmarsh was alive in 840 AD. One surviving charter of this date, from the reign of Beorhtwulf, the last fully independent king of Mercia, concerns land at Bromyard. In it, Bishop Cudwulf of Hereford grants the Ældorman Ælfstan about 500 acres of land by the River Frome for 'three lives' (i.e. a leasehold arrangement for Ælfstan's life and those of his next two heirs). The annual rent, to be paid to help support the mother church at Bromyard, reveals the surplus that could be generated from fertile land, over and above the needs of those who lived there. It was set at fifteen measures (a full butt) of unclouded ale, a hive-full of honey or its value in mead, one plough team of oxen, a hundred loaves, one sheep and one pig.[44]

By the time of the Domesday Survey in 1086, this estate seems to have been returned to the church, as Bishop Cudwulf had expected. Bromyard was recorded as having 30 hides of land belonging to the canons of Hereford (about 3,500 acres), although 3 of these hides had been unproductive since 1066: it is not clear whether this was due to Welsh raids, or to damage inflicted in the early years of Norman rule. Even so, it was a valuable holding, rated at the huge sum of £45.10s. for taxation purposes. It had a mill, large areas of fertile and productive meadows, woodland and a substantial population, at least 64 adult males plus an unknown

---

43 D Whitelock, *English Historical Documents 500-1042* (2 edn; London and New York: Routledge, 1979), p. 488, no. 62

44 Reproduced in P Williams, *Bromyard: Minster, Manor and Town* (Bromyard: Bromyard and District Local History Society, 1987), Plate I

number of 'their men', which could be a dozen or more.[45] There is, however, a difficulty with interpreting the Bromyard Domesday entry, since it is not clear what area it covers. There is no mention anywhere, for example, of Brockhampton or Whitbourne, which may be included under Bromyard. Conversely, two small estates which are now part of Winslow township in Bromyard, seem to be listed elsewhere in the survey. 120 acres at Rowden were held by King William himself, with a tenant farmer called Grimkel, perhaps the son of Grim who had farmed the land in 1066. Grimkel's farm had one plough team, and at least two families of dependent labourers, either Saxons or perhaps descendants of Viking settlers.[46] Secondly, Roger de Lacy (whose vast Lordship included 20,000 acres in Herefordshire), held a small estate called Cuple, which may correspond to the modern farm of Keephill. It was farmed by a man named Eadric, who had taken it over from the free tenant Leofsige. Eadric had two plough teams, and this hint of quite intensive land-use may explain how the value of his holding had increased from 5s. to 12s. in the 20 years since 1066. As well as having two dependent labouring families, Eadric owned three slaves.[47]

What was life like for these people a thousand years ago? The presence of slaves on farms, while Norman lords like Roger de Lacy owned great swathes of the country, shows that society was far from equitable. Not all slavery was for life, though: some were foreign captives, perhaps bought at the slave market from Viking traders at Bristol docks; others might be local people who had been unable to survive a harsh winter alone, and had sold themselves to the land-owners in exchange for housing and food. Also, some Saxon wills stipulated that slaves were to be given their freedom when the owner died. While there was slavery and poverty, there was also a legal system, and some sort of justice was available for all. Anglo-Saxon law codes survive from 600 AD, from the earliest years of the Saxon kingdoms, setting out detailed fines and punishments for all manner of crimes from theft to molesting women to murder. The ancient manors, small farmers and the old system of justice based on the local area and sworn juries, continued after the Norman Conquest, even though most of the major pre-Conquest landowners were either exiled or dead, replaced by men such as de Lacy.

One example of a law-suit shortly before the Conquest shows how well the system could work. It relates to a Herefordshire shire meeting at Ægelnothesstan (now Aylestone, in the suburbs of Hereford). The bishop, sheriff and other important men were present, and Edwin, a Welshman's son, came and brought a charge against his mother for withholding land from him at Wellington and Cradley. The bishop discovered that Thurkil the White, the man who should have represented Edwin's mother, could not give the details of the case, so three other thegns set off to speak to her. When they found her, she was furious with her son, summoned her relation Leofflaed, who in a farcical twist turned out to be married to Thurkil the White, and swore that she had granted no land to her son and never would. Instead, Leofflaed was to inherit everything, not only the land but jewellery, clothes and all. When the three thegns returned to the shire meeting at Aylestone, they

45 A Williams and G H Martin, ed., *Domesday Book: A Complete Translation* (2 edn; London: Penguin, 2003), p. 503, f. 182 V
46 *Ibid.* , p. 500, f. 181 R. Rowden is just north of Bromyard, on the River Frome
47 *Ibid.* , p. 510, f. 185 R

announced what they had found, and their word was accepted. Thurkil, who was presumably delighted and relieved at this outcome, obtained permission from the bishop to go to the cathedral and record it in the great bible there, as a precaution. This story, which shows gender equality at work as well as the role of the church in seeing justice done, is confirmed by a note in the ancient gospels at Hereford and also in Domesday Book, where part of Wellington is recorded as once being held by 'Thorkil White'.[48]

Despite the general scarcity of early documents for Herefordshire, the county is blessed with a unique manuscript, the so-called 'Herefordshire Domesday', which was probably written between 1160 and 1170. These years marked a turning point in the history of the Marches, after the decades of anarchy and wars between the royal cousins Stephen and Matilda (1135-54), and the suppression of Welsh raiders early in the reign of Matilda's son, Henry II. King Henry seems to have wanted to discover who had succeeded to the various lordships in Herefordshire, and so he had a copy of the county Domesday made which was then used as a template. This still survives, with marginal notes and jottings on the end pages, in a variety of hands, trying to explain how things had changed over the previous century. The most obvious feature for Bromyard (which a marginal comment shows is now spelled 'Bromiarde') is that it was largely business as usual, with the church still in possession of the main manors. Roger de Lacy, however, had backed William the Conqueror's eldest son Robert as the rightful heir to the throne, in unsuccessful uprisings in both 1088 and 1095. As a result, his lands had been forfeited to his younger brother Hugh, and later divided. Significantly perhaps for our understanding of these times, neither the land at Cuple farmed by Eadric, nor Leofflaed and Thurkil's inheritance at Wellington, merit a comment from the royal scribes. They were more interested in the major landholdings than the little local people.[49]

For detailed information about ordinary folk, we have to look at the records kept for rents and taxation. Wherever a landowner could gain financially from what they held, lists were made, and many of these have survived. This was, after all, the major purpose in producing the original Domesday Survey. The church, with its large estates passed down from bishop to bishop in an unbroken chain, was particularly keen on keeping such evidence. And so, there still exists a wonderful manuscript containing a detailed survey of the Hereford episcopal lands and tenants, dating to about 1285. Known as *The Red Book*, it supplies the earliest record of the people of the Bromyard area, including Studmarsh, dividing the parish into the town and its outlying districts (the 'foreign') (plate 11).[50] Careful study of the names used suggests that Bromyard foreign is set out in a geographical sequence; it is not possible to be precise, but this does seem to reflect the division into Linton, Norton and Winslow which occurs in later documents. It is suddenly possible to look in some detail at Linton and Norton, where Studmarsh is located, and to get a sense of its people in their setting. At an even more local level,

---

48 Whitelock, *E.H.D. 500-1042*, pp. 602-603, no.135; Williams and Martin, ed., *Domesday Book*, p. 516, f. 187 R

49 V H Galbraith and J Tait, ed., *Herefordshire Domesday, Circa 1160-1170* (The Pipe Roll Society; London: 1950)

50 The Red Book, *circa* 1285: HRO; BDLHS AW. B56/1/37-45

there are places where we seem to be concerned with the occupants of particular hamlets: Hodesbache (five separate tenants), Cuple (four tenants) or Ersete (two), all of which have been traced to modern farms, at Hodgebatch, Keephill and Yearsett.[51] On the other hand, we must beware of identifying people's names too closely with the place they currently lived. In these times before surnames, someone might equally well be known by their place of origin, for example the so-called William of Malvern. It is possible, but unlikely, that this free tenant with his modest landholding was some sort of minor absentee with a sub-tenant; more likely he was known to have come from the edge of Worcestershire to settle in Bromyard.

Thus *The Red Book* begins to bring the lives of the ordinary folk into clearer view, even though interpreting it is rather complex. Because the bishop was chiefly interested in his rents, the manuscript is arranged by type of tenant: those owing knight service (an agreement to supply a knight when required by the bishop), free tenants (who paid with an annual rent) and customary tenants (who also owed labour and other 'customs of the manor'). Linton had two tenants by knight service, but each were only liable for a part of a knight's fee. Bishops needed to be able to supply a small corps of troops when demanded by the king: in the days before regular national taxes or a standing army, knight service was one of the best ways of achieving this. In border dioceses like Hereford, the bishop was particularly responsible for combating Welsh incursions, and his men sometimes played a vital role in this. (Note that friction on the border is always described in Herefordshire as a Welsh incursion!). The two men holding by knight service in Linton were known as Robert of Brockhampton and Roger of Evesham, and were probably thought of as the most important residents of the township. Robert of Brockhampton may have lived somewhere in the centre of the modern Brockhampton estate, perhaps near Lower Brockhampton House, but Roger of Evesham almost certainly lived at Clater, near the crest of the main road into Bromyard.[52] We might note in passing that 'Caple' and 'Welintone' were other estates held from the bishop by knight service.

According to *The Red Book*, Robert and Richard of Brockhampton (perhaps brothers?) together held a hide of land (over 100 acres), and an additional acre of newly-claimed assart on Bringsty. An ancestor of theirs may perhaps have been the person who built the chapel at Brockhampton: certainly in 1283 Richard of Brockhampton sold the right of presentation there, which implies he was the patron. Robert still held his hide of land in 1304 but by 1383 John Domulton had taken it over, probably by marriage. The other main landholder, Roger of Evesham at Clater, held about 200 acres in all, some of it in Whitbourne parish; after his death it may have passed to his son Reginald.[53]

51 Williams, *Bromyard* , pp. 11, 32-33, 125-6, 137
52 Ibid. , pp. 122, 126, 129-30
53 W W Capes, ed., *Registrum Ricardi De Swinfield, Episcopi Herefordensis A.D. 1283-1317* (2 vols.; The Registers of the Bishops of Hereford; Hereford: Canterbury and York Society, 1909); R G Griffiths, ed., *Registrum Thome De Cantilupo, Episcopi Herefordensis A.D. 1275-1282* (2 vols.; The Registers of the Bishops of Hereford; Hereford: Canterbury and York Society, 1906)

Below these families in the pecking order were the freeholders, and below them again were the customary tenants, people much closer to our idea of serfs, with their obligation to work the manorial land as well as their own small acreages. The names represent separate tenant households liable for rent, so in order to get an idea of the total population we have to multiply by an estimate of average household size. This figure is hard to derive, since it has to take account of families as well as adults living alone, but 4.7 is one commonly used multiplier, rather higher than we would use for modern Britain. Four of the most interesting names in the freeholders list are Margaret and Hugh of Stubmarshe, Matilda of Stobmershe and Walter of Stubmershe. These four households each held a plot of land in the manor and it is noteworthy that two of them were headed by women, probably widows. Since surnames were not in use at this time, there is no particular reason to suppose that they were related directly, although it is likely that they had known each other for many years. Significantly, two of these, Margaret and Hugh, seem to be living in Norton, while Matilda and Walter are from the Linton part of the listings. This does suggest that the township boundary, which cuts across the project site today, ran through a recognisable hamlet in the 1280s. As noted above, however, we must not leap to conclusions about the size of the settlement at Studmarsh at this time, even if these various spellings do refer to our area of land. In the section of *The Red Book* which deals with Bromyard town, two other names stand out as a warning: William of Stobmarsh and Sibilla of Stobmarsh, both of whom owned land or houses at the beginning of what is now the Tenbury Road. Had these people acquired houses and moved into Bromyard itself, their nicknames relating to this origin 'out of town'? Or is it possible that while they paid rent for these plots in town, they normally lived out at Studmarsh, but had no rent obligations for land there?

There are some other people in *The Red Book* who are relevant to the story of Studmarsh. Half a mile to the east, there is a small area of land called The Orchards. It is now in Whitbourne parish, but until the Divided Parishes Act tidied up the boundaries in the nineteenth century it was a detached part of Linton. In 1285, this land was held by Gilbert of Coumbeye, another free tenant. He had half a virgate of land (1/8 of a hide, or about 15 acres), and after his time it became known as Combey's Land. Also in the list of freehold tenants is John of Brocampton, who held half a virgate, while the customary tenants include William of Brochampton and the Hardyesque Gilbert of Ok.

There are no Colleys or Biddles listed in *The Red Book* under Bromyard foreign, although it is impossible to know whether their bloodlines were already present when people are listed under names which include William son of Sibille (a customary tenant). There was a free tenant called Roger le Justice in Norton, which may be an occupational title, a nickname or an early inherited name. For Whitbourne, however, *The Red Book* lists Alfred the Beadle and William the Beadle as customary tenants, each holding six acres. We cannot be sure whether these are the ancestors of the Studmarsh Biddles, but it is at least possible.

What *The Red Book* does reveal is the pressure that was being put on the available land, as the population rose in the generally favourable climatic and social conditions of the thirteenth century. Names like Peter of Bryngsty and Walter of Baddeliche suggest there were already established encroachments into the old commons of Bringsty and Badley Wood. Moreover, a series of rents for assarts show the trend was continuing and probably intensifying in an effort to grown enough grain. Some 33 acres of assart had been cut into these commons from the Bromyard side, including twelve acres claimed by Matilda of Stobmershe and one acre by Walter. Although this indicates a growing population and suggests a superficial prosperity, the increasing depletion of the commons, which were so vital for wood and for feeding pigs in the autumn, was not sustainable without major changes to the agricultural system used. But innovations of this kind usually need surplus wealth and space to experiment, neither of which existed in this time of increasing land-hunger.

Chapter 5. The Mind of the Past: Trauma and Recovery

Some periods in the past seem pivotal, either as major breaks with what went before or turning points that mark the way for the future. These times may be quite brief, a single battle or one Act of Parliament, or they may be longer-lasting, deeper-rooted, more fundamental. One such epoch-making time was the fourteenth century. This was, above all others, a century of trauma focussed on the plague known as the Black Death, a disaster that eventually shaped the way ahead, out of the middle ages. These were years of catastrophic change on a scale it is hard to comprehend and almost impossible to underestimate. In crude numbers alone, this was a century of population decline – of death – of shattering proportions. The worst episode in our own collective memory may be the losses commemorated on war memorials all over Britain, which can provide a bench-mark. To equate with the fourteenth-century cataclysm, the 1914-1919 British dead would have been not 1.2 million but 12 million, ten times the percentage mortality.

The events of the fourteenth century go far beyond the apocalyptic loss of life. The changes visited on Studmarsh and a thousand places like it are tangible, felt through the soles of your feet as you walk across the ground; they took place in the fields and villages of our localities. They are visible, in the ruins of houses where the signs of the past remain; in the bend of tracks and country lanes that now skirt hollow, empty fields; in the recovered traces of charcoal and pottery in the soil, and in the written word. Not least, the consequences of this century of trauma were profoundly spiritual, in the challenge they hurled at the established understanding of faith, law and order; these challenges outlived the century of their birth and they still have power today, in the cries of lost communities and dislocated lives; these were in a real sense our ancestors, our people.

Few periods of our history have so much power to evoke a response, when the people caught up in the unfolding disaster seem to speak directly to us over the years. This is empathy born of helplessness: the succession of crises were visited on the people, without their having done anything to deserve it, and without any means to turn the tide.

The mental health recovery model, with its holistic approach looking at the whole person in their situation and carefully exploring the past, has much to offer when we are reflecting on these tempestuous changes. The fourteenth century was the focus of the archaeological element of the project; the most likely time at which the population of Studmarsh might have declined, when disaster might have struck the little community; the century for which the most significant finds might be uncovered. But the methods of the recovery model can take us wider than this. The processes involved in the Studmarsh investigations were always going to have parallels with any journey of discovery, whether physical, academic or internal. Even though each of the project disciplines have their own methodologies and support systems, the outcomes were 'unknowns' until the research was complete. Just as mental ill-health provokes fear of the unknown, a fear which the project helped to address, so Past in Mind encouraged the three disciplines to collaborate in meeting the unknown history of the site.

A particularly powerful parallel with the personal recovery model is that the thirteenth-century population of Studmarsh, with their beliefs and ways of life, cannot and have not been re-created, put back as we have glimpsed them in 1285 in *The Red Book,* in the days before the famines took hold. No more can we return to the way of life during the Anglo-Saxon take-over, or to before the Norman Conquest, nor undo any of the other seismic changes that have been explored in earlier chapters. What has happened, however, is that the project participants have 'got to know' these communities of the past, and in the process have encountered these ancestral lives as they were affected by events experienced centuries ago. And in so doing, there has been an offer made, hands extended, to engage with these past lives and reflect on their shared journeys.

Social inclusion was one of the basic premises of the project and one of its major successes, providing as it did a model for integrating all the contributing groups. Yet this is one of the biggest differences between the project tenets and the harshest years of the fourteenth century. Plague sufferers were very unlikely to be welcomed into other communities, rather they would have been isolated, shunned and excluded. To a lesser extent, famine victims would have faced the same discrimination, and struggled to find food or even shelter outside their own parish, except in religious houses. No other social mechanism existed for distributing food, so those who had grain tended to hoard it, and those who had money bought up what they could. At a time of great need, those already suffering the most would have found themselves forced further into the margins of society. Whereas Past in Mind set out to minimise labelling people as 'what' and instead named and recognised them as individuals, the fourteenth-century crisis probably heightened existing tendencies to hostile identification of strangers as 'other'.

The grass is green again now in Studmarsh; it has returned to being a meadow. Scars of the past and of the project excavations alike seem healed, although the houses and previous lives are still past and gone. Careful backfilling has laid the discoveries made there to rest again while the knowledge gained can be built on. It has enabled the grass sward to recover and the meadow to be used again for grazing, sward which had to be fenced off while the project was underway but now is all part of the meadow again. What has survived, to join the other discovered echoes of past occupants, is a memory of the community that flourished there while the older history was uncovered.

The difference at the Studmarsh dig was that backfilling was part of the process, and one of the most important parts. A task which is often good-humoured but normally aims to leave the turf level, trampling down the soil to compact it, to finish the job and go home, became a reverent homage to the stories that had been found and the human lives that had been uncovered. The putting back of the pieces became a symbolic restoration, in tune with the wider goal of understanding and respecting the lives of the past. Each stone, each shovel of soil, was carefully replaced as if the jagged edges of history were being laid back to rest. The disturbed land was not to be subjected to additional trauma. For the professional archaeologists, this was a transformative experience, an engagement with new vistas into the story of the site.

Plate 17. Danse Macabre Nottingham alabasters in Holy Trinity Church, Cherbourg, portraying Death dancing with the king of France and with a beggar.

Plate 18. The plague cross in Ross on Wye churchyard, commemorating the plague victims of 1637.

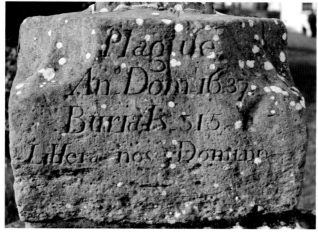

Plate 19. Top. Albrecht Dürer's woodcut of The Four Horsemen of the Apocalypse (1498) vividly portrays the horrific events of the fourteenth and fifteenth centuries, as Famine, Pestilence, War and Death ride heedlessly into people's lives. (Metropolitan Museum of Art, New York, © Photo *SCALA*, Florence, 2014) Bottom. Close up of the cross inscription at Ross, begging God for mercy.

Plate 20. The lively fifteenth-century misericord seats at Ripple in Worcestershire hint at the better conditions that slowly emerged in England. Top: pig-killing in November; bottom: spinning by the fire in December.

Plate 21. With less pressure on the land, many farmers were able to experiment with new enterprises. Top: dove cotes provided additional protein and variety, and bird-scaring became correspondingly important; bottom: the blessing of the land at Rogation was a major community event.

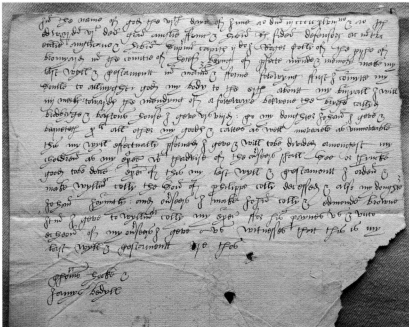

Plate 22. Top. Swithin Butterfield's beautifully-written survey of Bishop Scory's estates, carried out in the 1570s, contains detailed information about land holdings in many parishes in Herefordshire, including Bromyard. Bottom. Roger Colley's will of 1548 was the earliest document of its kind that we used. Roger's name appears towards the right-hand end of line three, and James Biddle was one of the two witnesses. Significantly for such an early date, James was able to sign his name.

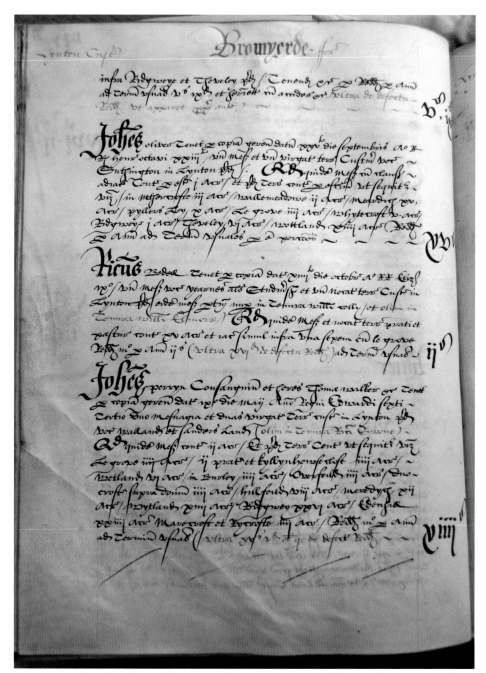

Plate 23. In the middle of this page of Butterfield's survey, we read that Richard Biddle held a house (messuage) called Yearnes, alias Studmarsh, which was tenanted by William Colley.

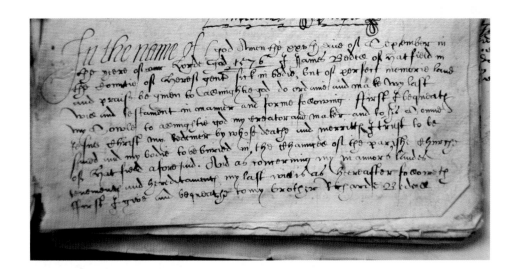

Plate 24. In his will of 1576, James Biddle left to his brother Richard Biddle (bottom of page one), property called Combey's and Studmarsh with all their 'messuages, landes, tenements, meadows, leasowes, pastures and woods' (top of page two).

Plate 25. One of James Biddle's other properties was Gaines, now Old Gaines, in the neighbouring parish of Whitbourne. If, as seems likely, this was the house which still stands, its huge fireplace and elegantly-beamed ceilings would have been added some time after James' death. His house would probably have been open to the rafters.

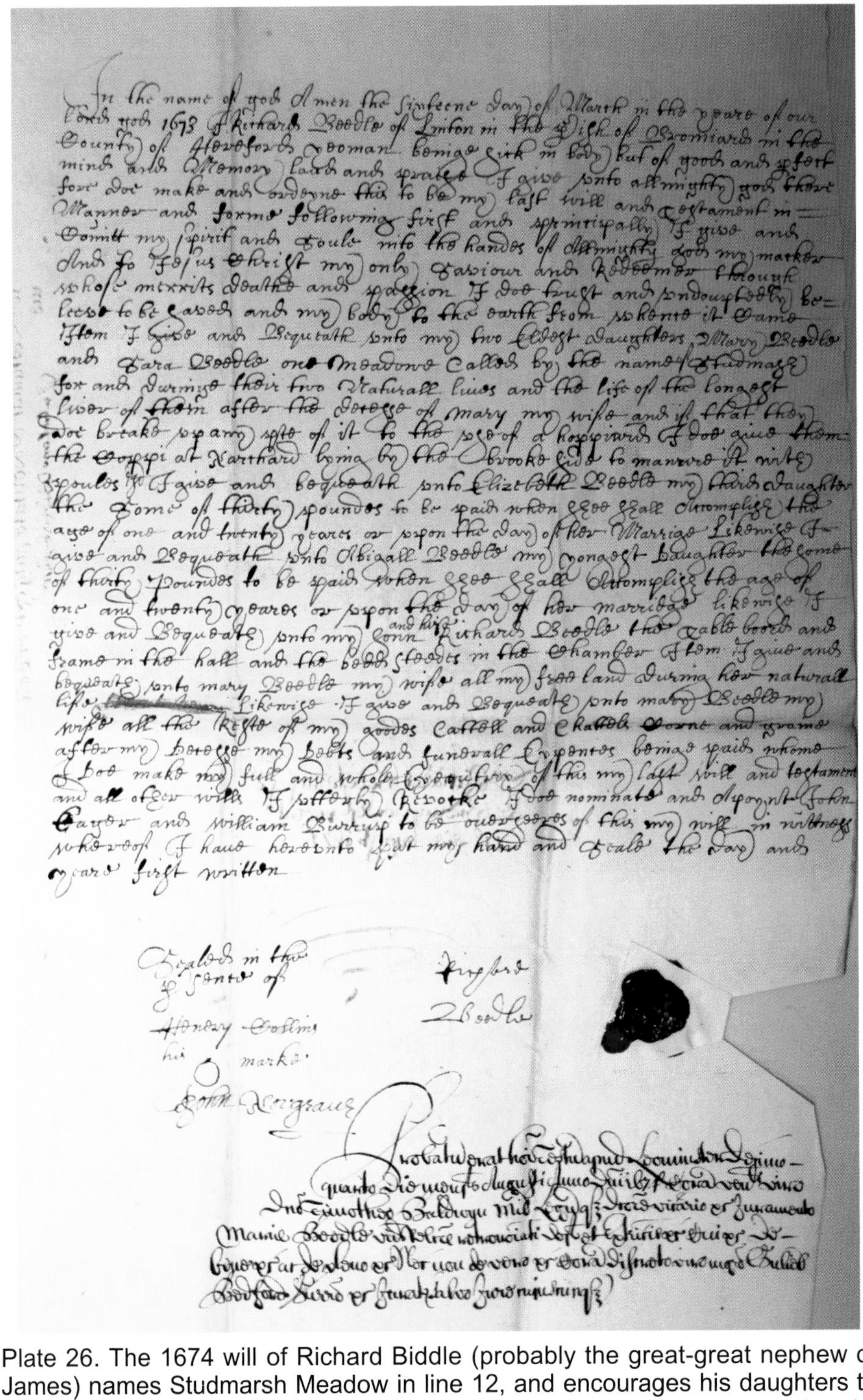

Plate 26. The 1674 will of Richard Biddle (probably the great-great nephew of James) names Studmarsh Meadow in line 12, and encourages his daughters to begin growing hops with the promise of 'the coppi of Narchard lying by the brook'. His youngest daughter was called Abigail, the first member of the family with that name.

An Inventorie of all the goods and Chattells
late of Richard Beedle of Linton in the Wish of
Bromiard in the County of Hereford Yeoman
deceased taken valued and prized the Thirteenth
day of July in the yeare of our Lord god 1674
by us John Bayer James Fowtie William
Burrop Edward Colly John Norgrave as
followeth

	£	s	d
Imprimis his wearinge Apparrell	1	6	8
Item in the Hall one Table bord and frame two Chaires one forme one Joype Cubard	0	13	4
Lining of all sortes	3	0	0
Item two fether Beeds and one florck beed	2	0	0
Item three bed steeds and three Coffers	1	0	0
Item fower Blankets one Coverleede two thrum Clothes	1	0	0
Brass and Pewter of all sortes	2	0	0
Item provision of all sortes	1	0	0
Item two Kill heares	0	5	0
Item hoggsheds and other Coupery ware	1	0	0
Item one Sider mill	0	16	0
Item three Acres of Rye	2	10	0
Item fower Acres of Lent graine	1	6	8
Item Hay	1	10	0
Item three bullockes	6	0	0
Item two Kine	4	5	0
Item two yeare old beese and 2 Calves	3	0	0
Item one old mare	1	10	0
Item three Ewes and Lames	0	15	0
Item Imployments of husbandry of all sortes and other Lumber forgotten	0	10	0

James Fowtie
John Bayer
his I marke   the totall is 35 — 7 — 8

William Burrop
his S marke   apprized
Edward Colly
his A marke

John Norgrave

Plate 28. Top. Small pieces of blackware (TP3 002) and combed yellow ware (TP2 002) contemporary with Richard Biddle and his children were found near the top of two test pits. Combed yellow-ware was typically used for plates and shallow bowls. Bottom. Black-ware was often used as mugs and small cups, such as this almost-complete example found in Shropshire. (Portable Antiquities Scheme)

Plate 29. The final event of the project celebrated the life of Studmarsh and its people. Top: belief in the future was personified by Richard Biddle; bottom left: the Black Death did its worst; bottom right: Abigail and the hopeful young visitor.

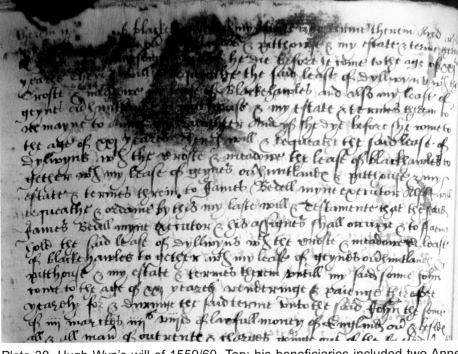

Plate 30. Hugh Wyn's will of 1559/60. Top: his beneficiaries included two Anne Biddles, daughters of Robert and Walter (lines 11 and 14); bottom: he appointed James Biddle as his executor (line 13), to manage his estate including 'Geynes and Huntlandes' (line 15).

Plate 31. Top. Towards the end of his will, Hugh Wyn describes James Biddle as 'my especiall trustie ffrende & kinsman' (line 5). Bottom. The historical research was mostly done in the Hereford Record Office or here in the Bromyard and District Local History Centre.

Plate 32. Despite what they say, it didn't rain every day in summer 2012. (Past in Mind archive)

Life at Studmarsh : Houses and House-platforms

The archaeological fieldwork concentrated on signs of previous human habitation, to access the lives of former inhabitants. It looked at areas of the project site where there was no obvious sign of 'life', but where to the experienced eye there seemed to be a good chance that something might be discovered. There were three main stages: a full-site survey, digging of test pits and then excavating larger trenches. Each of these phases made their own distinctive contribution.

The initial task was a detailed site survey, exploring the whole project area to become familiar with it, and then conducting a detailed technical survey. This part of the work is always more challenging than expected, as people compare what they are learning with pre-existing knowledge and expectations, even learning new ways of learning. It is also a time when the people on the dig really begin to get to know each other as individuals, developing the project community despite the inclement weather, difficult terrain and other obstacles.

Out of this survey work came two important outcomes. Firstly, the old tracks that served the settlement were identified and mapped. The main one, worn down into a significant hollow way, must have been the route most often used by earlier inhabitants. It divided the settlement in two, giving access to and from the main road and the common, between what is now the ruined cottage and its garden. Along most of its length through the research area, this hollow way forms the boundary between the ancient townships of Linton and Norton, suggesting that it might have been a well-trodden path for many centuries. As well as this main track, two smaller ones were identified and mapped, branching off roughly at right angles from it.

Secondly the platforms, many of which could have been for housing, were surveyed, including four which had not been identified before (see plate 12). An earlier superficial look at the site had found several platforms, three of which were thought to have been associated with buildings. All these had been described as post-medieval, in other words more recent that about 1540. To these we can add the cottage and garden by the hollow way, which was occupied into the early twentieth century but is now ruined, and the still-occupied Grove Farm. All but two of the previously-identified platforms (the ruined cottage site and a flat area on the damp ground at the head of Bond's Dingle) were in Norton. During the survey work, a further four platforms were identified, all tentatively dated to the medieval and post-medieval periods, 1066 onwards. Three were in Linton, to the west of the upper section of the hollow way, the fourth was in Norton, on the high ground along the eastern edge of the site. In other words, this survey work expanded the possibilities for understanding the site in two ways: it spread the area of potential settlement further into Linton, and it shifted the possible dates earlier by five hundred years, by fitting the observations into other known information.

Following the survey, six test pits were dug. This was the moment when the group really began to gel, not least because of the shared experience of the torrential rain, the mud and the camaraderie arising from the other inconveniences of the site. Test pitting is the time when you learn the discipline of disturbing the veneer of sward and soil to see what is below, digging down into the past and recognising what is there. You discover how to interpret the soil layer by layer, learning to go slowly and take time to appreciate the evidence you uncover. There is a moment when you discover that soil is not just mud, but a complex structure of textures, colours and fabric which hold clues to the land's past. And then any finds made need relating to other sites, to pre-existing standards and examples, and they have to be saved, protected and understood.

Three of the test pits were in Norton. One (TP 5), near a minor hollow way, produced no finds all the way down to the natural base of compacted red clay. The other two Norton pits (TP 4 and 6) both came down onto stones and were later extended into trenches; TP 6 also produced a single sherd of medieval jug, tentatively dated to the fourteenth century.[54] The other three test pits were in Linton, just below the eastern end of the hollow way. Two of these failed to reach the natural, because there was such a depth of old plough soil. One of these two (TP 2) produced 42 sherds dating back to the seventeenth century, the other (TP 3) produced four sherds, two of which were seventeenth- or eighteenth-century and the other two were pieces of medieval cooking pots (plates 14 and 15). The last test pit in Linton did go down to the natural base clay, but the sherds found in it could not be reliably dated.

Hindsight is a wonderful thing. As the historical research unfolded it became increasingly apparent that test pits in the enclosure of the ruined cottage and at The Grove might have uncovered helpful evidence.[55] But as with life in general, there are always limits to what is achievable; in this particular case the constraints of funding, time and foul weather played decisive roles. Selection of test pit locations may well have affected what was discovered, but this was in turn partly determined by the direction taken in the initial historical investigations. Preconceptions, prejudices and decisions at the outset all impacted on later outcomes. Test pit 3, for example, had only produced four sherds of pottery when it was abandoned at nearly a meter in depth. It was 'too difficult' and so was left incomplete. But two of those four sherds were medieval: what else lies undiscovered in the layers below? Had we come close to important material? How can we discern when to stop trying and move on elsewhere?

The third phase of the field work involved further excavation of selected areas, especially on two of the housing platforms which were considered likely to be particularly productive. Test pits 6 and 4, which had both been halted when they uncovered stone work which might have once formed part of a building, were extended into trenches (named T1 and T2 respectively). Trench 3 was to examine the sequence of rectangular surface features in the meadow, but it produced no conclusive evidence.

---

54 D Williams and C Atkinson, 'Studmarsh Medieval Settlement, Brockhampton, Herefordshire: A Summary Report on Excavations in August 2012' in *Herefordshire Archaeology Reports* (Hereford: Herefordshire Archaeology, 2013), p. 47
55 Casual finds of medieval pottery at The Grove do seem to substantiate this. S. Palmer, *pers. comm.*

Trench 2 was the smaller of the two, and despite careful work it remained hard to interpret. Evidence was found for the remains of two walls, rough floor surfaces and a post hole, and it seemed probable that the site had been levelled into a small terrace before it was built on. The excavation also found some stones which could have come from a more robust building, and several pieces of fired clay daub. It was not clear if the building was domestic, or a small extension to a larger dwelling nearby, or some other building close to a more substantial one. Unfortunately, no readily-datable artefacts were found in this trench, so its age remains unclear.

Trench 1 by contrast revealed clear evidence for a building with large stone foundations, which seems to have been used for human habitation for at least part of its life (plate 16). This trench was extended eventually to 6 x 2m with three small additional trenches nearby to try and clarify the overall size of the building, although this was only partially successful. The building appears to have been about 5.5m long, with at least one internal division which was probably made with a timber partition. The most substantial wall found was at the south-eastern end; this wall was about 0.8m wide, faced on both sides and set on rubble footings 2m wide and 0.45m deep. It was, in other words, a very solid construction, made with considerable care. Mid-way along this main wall there was what appeared to have been a doorway, which had been loosely filled in with stone at some stage: there were no footings here, which probably explains why the fill was unstable and had later collapsed into the building.

Associated with the building discovered in this trench, among the footings stones and immediately outside the walls, there were several sherds of pottery, mostly dated to the thirteenth and fourteenth centuries. There were also some Roman pieces and some which could not definitely be dated more closely than 'Roman, possibly Iron Age or up to 14th century'. No roofing stones or tiles were found, which were initially anticipated because of the higher than expected status of the construction methods used in the building; this absence was at first attributed to robbing out of materials from the site. But it is also possible that, despite the well-made walls, the roof could have been thatched.[56] This evolving understanding of the building, and hence of the lives of its occupants, is a classic illustration of the iterative nature of both historical and archaeological investigations, the need to revisit previous conclusions and modify them in the light of new evidence, a process which sits so well with mental health recovery.

The interpretation of the important building discovered here is still not complete. Because there were fragments of pottery dated to the thirteenth and fourteenth centuries in the main wall footings, it has been called 'medieval'. The absence of any pottery of early modern date, together with the presence of a mature oak close by, suggests that the building probably went out of use in or about the sixteenth century. But what of the Roman (and possibly Iron Age) pottery found? How much more might have been discovered if the medieval building had been dismantled and its site excavated further? It was thought that these walls rested on the natural substrate, so to excavate further would destroy more than might be gained. Is this reason enough to halt there? How far back into the past do we want and need to

---

56 Williams and Atkinson, 'Studmarsh Medieval Settlement' , section report, Baker, N, pp. 50-51

go when trying to understand the past life of a house and its occupants? It would take courage to unpick the neat medieval walls, to delve down earlier and risk what might or might not by chance be found.

The problem we face in Herefordshire is the extreme scarcity of excavations of this type. Despite the numerous deserted and shrunken settlements known to exist in the county, only one or two others have been excavated, and only partially so. The same is true of Shropshire, which in many ways has a similar medieval history. So there is very little comparative data, and it is impossible to evaluate and contextualise what may have been found. A comparison with an excavation at Hampton Wafer, which is the only other significant excavation so far carried out in Herefordshire, suggests that most buildings might have had a succession of alterations and re-builds over the centuries, and these remodellings would not always have been on exactly the same footprint. The blocked-in doorway found at Studmarsh may be an example of this sort of 'make-over', and one might perhaps go so far as to speculate that the deep footings were added on the down-hill side, including by chance some relatively late sherds of pottery, if the house had been expanded at some point. Equally, it is possible that our house may have had an earlier, predominantly timber, phase before the one we discovered.[57]

When all is said and done, the 'success' of this dig has to be that it happened at all, rather than in precise or quantifiable interpretation of its results. It has too few parallels for assessment in these terms. This is arguably true of its archaeological and historical value and also of the value of Past in Mind as a whole.

More than Numbers

The archaeological survey suggested evidence for as many as fifteen places in Studmarsh (including the ruined cottage site and the still-occupied house called The Grove) where there may have been buildings in the pre-modern period.

What does this mean in human terms? Assuming for now that all of these were at one stage occupied simultaneously, and that each had an 'average' sized household, we can get an estimate of the maximum possible number of people who might once have lived in this hamlet. Using the same standard multiplier of 4.7 which we used in the previous chapter, this would mean that Studmarsh could theoretically have had a population of about 70 at its absolute peak, compared with just one person living there now. Of course, several of the platforms were probably for other purposes than human habitation, or may have been used in succession, so this is likely to be an over-estimate, but the comparison with today is still instructive. It is worth remembering, however, that population levels can change very fast, apparently by chance alone: quite recently there were many more people in the last two houses to be occupied here. A family of five lived at The Grove in the 1980s, and even the ruined cottage was occupied into the twentieth century.

---

57 S.C Stanford, 'The Deserted Medieval Village of Hampton Wafer, Herefordshire', *Transactions of the Woolhope Naturalists' Field Club* 39 (1967): 71-92; Baker, N, in Williams and Atkinson, 'Studmarsh Medieval Settlement' , pp. 50-51

It is almost impossible to get a reliable picture of the changing number of people living in Studmarsh or even in Linton and Norton, over a long span of years. In Domesday Book, the entry for Bromyard includes several other parishes, probably underestimates the numbers associated with the mother church in the town and has a cryptic reference to an unknown number of 'their men', some of whom may have had families. The listed population in 1086 equates to about 300, but we can only use this as a very rough guide. Nor does the estimation of numbers living in and around Bromyard get any easier later on. True, Bromyard becomes divided into borough and foreign, but the division is not exact. The modern town has spread out across part of Winslow township in the old foreign, the modern censuses vary in their sub-divisions, and in the 1285 *Red Book* the township boundaries are not made explicit. In many ways it is better to use a proxy for these calculations, and once the adjacent parish of Whitbourne appears in the records, it has much to recommend it for this purpose. Socially it was similar to the townships of Linton and Norton, and being rural it was likely to be faced with similar opportunities and pressures. Bromyard itself, by contrast, would later develop into a significant market town, with the associated chances and changes that rural parishes often missed.

The earliest opportunity we have to estimate the population of Whitbourne is in *The Red Book*, when it was about 480. The next figure comes from government records for a poll tax levied in 1377 on everyone aged 14 and over. This is a crucial date, being a whole generation after the first outbreak of the Black Death and also after many of the other horrors of the century. The multiplication factor to use is also more accurate, since the only unknowns are the number who avoided paying the tax and the proportion of young people in the population.[58] Using the best agreed methods, it seems that the population of Whitbourne in 1377 had fallen to about 140: less than a third of that ninety years earlier. The figures for the whole of Bromyard foreign suggest that the 1285 population of 670 had crashed to 170 in 1377 (a quarter); Studmarsh, as a small part of this area, was unlikely to have been significantly different. These medieval figures can be put in context with some more recent ones for Whitbourne. A church census of 1676 found that the population had only just recovered to pre-plague levels after three hundred years, with about 500 people of all ages resident;[59] the 1831 national census recorded 899 people, at or close to the highest ever in the parish, after which it fell as agricultural labourers left the land again. Unlike Studmarsh, Whitbourne has seen considerable modern growth so that in 2001 the population was up again, at 796.

This pattern is repeated across most parts of the English countryside, with communities either contracting permanently or shrinking for a hundred years or more before slowly recovering, often in slightly different places and certainly with new houses. There are no houses in Whitbourne which go back to the pre-plague era, but several of the finest and oldest ones were built in the period of restoration in its aftermath. These new houses might carry the same names as their medieval

---

58 C C Fenwick, ed., (Records of Social and Economic History; Oxford: The British Academy, 1998)
59 A Whiteman and M Clapinson, ed., *The Compton Census of 1676: A Critical Edition* (Records of Social and Economic History, N.S.; London: Oxford University Press, for The British Academy, 1986), p. 261

precursors, but they represent a new way of living, built in the new world after the crisis. Very few settlements seem to have been completely abandoned as a result of the events of the fourteenth century, and in many cases in Herefordshire they were probably always scattered, perhaps always slowly shifting as conditions and needs changed and challenges arose.

The extent of these changes, and the long time that places like Studmarsh and Whitbourne took to recover from the earlier devastation, is very visible in Swithin Butterfield's survey, made for the Bishop of Hereford in 1570s. The holdings of William Colley and William Huck in Whitbourne are typical of many.[60]

William Colley's customary land in the 1570s consisted of Marralls, his house by the mill at Sapey Bridge, with 7 acres, and a further two derelict house-sites known as Bylmings and Symons, with eight acres between them; these names might have been remembering the families who once lived there. Colley also held eleven other pieces of land, bringing his total holding to 50 acres. One acre, somewhere just south of the main road, is described as lying between the land belonging to 'the heirs of James Bedell and the heirs of Brockhampton'.

The entry after Mr Colley is for William Huck, who lived at Poswick, which still exists as a tiny hamlet close to Badley Wood Common. The description of the site 'bounded with the common way that leadeth from Rosemore unto Badleys on the west' makes it clear for those with local knowledge that the present green lane between the fields was then a regularly-used road: further evidence of adaptation and readjustment in the landscape over time. Like William Colley, Huck held two abandoned house-sites and their land, and other land adjacent to that of the heirs of James Bedell, or Biddle. In his case, however, there was a dispute over which pieces of land were his, which belonged to Bedell's heirs and which were held by the bishop as lord of the manor.

Although these two men were richer that some, the contrast with the situation 250 years earlier is revealing. *The Red Book* describes a landscape bursting at the seams, with fields and houses being carved out of the commons and people living cheek by jowl in the limited space available. Long after the century of trauma, Butterfield saw abandoned homes, farmsteads in ruins and settlements where multiple-ownership was the order of the day.

The Years of Trauma

Medieval people lived much 'closer to the edge' than we do now, and it can be hard to understand their habitual physical insecurity. For the vast majority of British people today, normal life pre-supposes enough food, winter warmth and access to doctors who can cure many day-to-day illnesses. Deviations from these norms are perceived as upsetting the proper course of life. For all but a tiny group at the top of medieval society, life was much less cushioned, and even for this elite the troubles brought by fickle rulers, war and disease were an ever-present reality. Winters brought regular hardship, and for most people there was always

---

60 Swithin Butterfield, ff. 115 R, 130 R and V; BDLHS He. L57

the lurking anticipation of the 'hungry gap', as summer came but the crops were not yet ripe, while stored food ran low. Until the broad bean harvest and the first feast, there was no guarantee of survival. Some years were worse than others, with poor harvests, epidemics or civil unrest making a hard life more marginal still. And then there were the major disasters, times of widespread famine, or pandemics like the Black Death when the world made no sense.

The real troubles began with cold summers and torrential rain in 1314-1317. Three abysmal harvests led to widespread famine, compounded by a disease which might have been poisoning from eating mouldy grain. Many sheep also died, perhaps from liver fluke. An estimated 10% of the population died in these years in the rural south, more in the towns and in the north of England where there was also vicious warfare. Many experts believe that this was the worst period of harvest failure across northern Europe in 2,000 years. Although 1319 was a dry year, recovery was halted because an epidemic (perhaps rinderpest) killed over half of all the cattle in England. With few plough-oxen, little milk or cheese and a shortage of manure, villages and people struggled to get back on their feet. After a generation's respite, the cattle murrain returned in 1346.[61]

The Black Death itself spread across mainland Europe during 1347 and 1348, while England prayed to be spared. In October 1348, Bishop Trilleck of Hereford was informed by the Bishop of London that the plague was approaching. But the letter had been accidentally delayed and by the time Herefordshire was alerted, the epidemic had reached England and begun to spread out from Dorset. By December deaths were occurring in Bristol, and the first recorded clerical death in Hereford diocese was in the spring of 1349. Frome deanery, the area which included Bromyard, was particularly badly hit. In all, just over half of all the parish priests in the diocese died during 1349, and many of these were victims of the plague.[62] It would be reasonable to assume only slightly lower fatality levels among the laity. The cause of this terrifying death rate was starkly simple: there had almost certainly been no outbreaks of plague in Britain for many centuries, and so the people had no immunity.

Twelve years later, the plague returned. This time it was especially cruel, picking off as if by choice babies and young children, cutting away the new shoots of life. From summer 1361 to May 1362 it circled like a carrion crow, then faded away, to return again in 1369 and in 1375. Now, however, there was some immunity in the population, and the next significant epidemic was not until August 1407.[63] Those who had recovered from the disease were unlikely to die at the next assault, but many young people, as yet untouched, died each time, and with every new outbreak the small and struggling hamlets and villages found it harder to start up again. Meanwhile, the plagues were becoming worse in towns and cities than in

61 P Slavin, 'The Great Bovine Pestilence and Its Economic and Environmental Consequences in England and Wales, 1318-50', *The Economic History Review* 65 (2012): 1239-66
62 J H Parry, ed., *Registrum Johanes De Trilleck, Episcopi Herefordensis A.D. 1344-1361* (2 vols.; The Registers of the Bishops of Hereford; Hereford: Canterbury and York Society, 1910), pp. 137-9; W J Dohar, *The Black Death and Pastoral Leadership: The Diocese of Hereford in the Fourteenth Century* (Philadelphia: University of Pennsylvania Press, 1995), p. 34
63 J H Parry, ed., *Registrum Roberti Mascall, Episcopi Herefordensis A.D. 1404-1417* (The Registers of the Bishops of Hereford; Hereford: Canterbury and York Society, 1917)

rural areas. Young adults were tending to leave the shrinking communities of the countryside, to find brighter prospects in the job market that was opened up for them in the towns. In a cruel twist, the relative youth of urban populations was itself part of the reason why their plague mortality was so high.

The later 1400s were relatively free of epidemics, but then the midlands experienced another major population collapse, averaging about a fifth between 1548 and 1563. The exact causes are not known, but fatalities were especially frequent in towns and were perhaps largely due to influenza and typhus, diseases typical of overcrowded and unhygienic places.[64] Bromyard is one of the few places in Britain which has parish registers going back to the 1530s, and they clearly show this high mortality. The population seems to have fallen by about a third, with several years of double the normal death rate. In the worst year recorded, 1545, the three months from August to October had half as many burials again as were normal in a whole year, while the total deaths for the year were three times the average. Perhaps significantly, there are no burial registrations for the years from 1554 to 1556: we cannot tell if this is coincidence, or if these unrecorded years were even worse.[65]

From 1570 to 1640, famine and plague returned to Herefordshire for what would prove to be their last attacks. Bromyard had an isolated crisis in 1573, when nine people died of plague in two months. In 1580 there was a bad outbreak in Hereford, with summer burials running at five times the normal rate, but this time Bromyard seems to have been spared. But then there were failed harvests in both 1586 and 1587, and there was so little grain that it had to be imported from Danzig and Hamburg. Again in the 1590s there were a run of bad harvests in many parts of England, culminating in a severe famine in 1597, when wheat prices doubled. Associated with this was an increase in itinerancy and begging, accompanied by widespread fears of unrest. In a society prone to xenophobia and a deep suspicion of wandering strangers, tolerance for needy outsiders, even if from only five miles away, was by no means the normal reaction. Indeed, harsh new legislation was passed against vagrancy at precisely this time, reinforcing a natural tendency to stigmatise and fear the unfamiliar.

In 1609-10, the plague was more widespread. In Bromyard, a 30% increase in mortality in 1609 was followed by a doubling in 1610; of the 66 burials listed that year, 24 are specifically attributed to 'pestilencia'. The situation at Hereford was so bad, and terror of the plague so great, that the assizes were moved to Leominster. Then the plague returned one more time, in 1635-7, although only one person was listed as a victim in Bromyard, and he was the vicar of nearby Wacton. In other places this last visitation was far worse. A cross in Ross churchyard indicates something of the horror and anguish it provoked there. It is dedicated to the 315 victims of the epidemic, out of a total population of about 1800, and bears the desperate plea 'Libera nos Domine' – Spare us, O Lord (plates 18 and 19).

---

64 J S Moore, 'The Mid-Tudor Population Crisis in Midland England, 1548-1563', *Midland History* 34 (2009): 44-57
65 BDLHS Bromyard Parish Registers

Counting the Cost, Finding New Paths

In so many ways, the people of the past were just like us, numb or weeping at gravesides, celebrating new births and good harvests, stopped with delight at spring birdsong and autumnal mist. But it has also been well said that the past is a foreign country[66], where mankind saw events very differently, and we look at it as if through tinted glass. We need to take time to understand their world before we can sympathise with their experiences.

The basis for medieval society was described as a threefold division of labour. The peasants worked the land and provided food; the knights and of course the king, anointed by God, defended the land from harm; and the clergy, monks and nuns prayed for God's blessing and provision. Even if the system was less good in practice than the theory suggests, there was a kind of divine symmetry and logic to it, with the whole of society meshing together for the common good.

The troubles which began in the fourteenth century shattered this safe icon, once and for all. The land failed to provide for the people despite their labours, civil order broke down and the prayers of the faithful were not answered. Plague deaths were particularly high among the most pastorally-caring clergy, those who visited the sick and buried the dead rather than abandoning their posts. Death struck in the monasteries, too. At Llanthony Priory near Gloucester, only four of its thirty occupants survived 1349. There was confusion as to whether the plague was a divine punishment for terrible sins, or whether a merciful God would lift it from his people.

Out of the chaos arose new ways of seeing the world. In the short term, the bishops continued to keep the old order going, ordaining new priests for the parish churches as fast as they could find candidates who met the minimum standards. But men and women alike discovered that there were no real bars to them moving to places with brighter prospects; higher wages were demanded and obtained; and there was far more social as well as geographical mobility. And the old belief-system, resting as it did on the foundations of reward for virtuous living, and the efficacy of penance and prayer through the saints for sins committed, failed utterly when challenged by the indiscriminate destruction of famine and plague.

When the bishop enquired into the state of the church in Bromyard in 1397, he found that it was not only the laity whose respect for the old traditions had waned. Even though the report is now partly illegible, it speaks of a community in confusion. Is it too much to read into it a hint that the community was also inclined to fix blame on one unusual woman, one person who did not follow expected patterns of behaviour?

> The Parishioners say the Vicar must find one candle for the high altar, day and night, because he does not do it. They also say the Vicar must find 4 processional candles for solemn days, but he only provides 2. Also that Stephen Brome owes 12d. obligatory payment towards the service for the blessed Mary for a plot of land which he occupies in

66 L P Hartley, *The Go-Between* (London: Penguin, 1953), p. 1

Bromyard. Also that Walter Godynge owes 12d. for the same service. Likewise Deyota de la Orcharde the same amount, and Walter Brugge the same amount as well.

They also say Alson Broune cursed some man with her own . . . from her evil invocation that God will take her own vengeance upon himself, and she has done this several times. This is against the Catholic faith and has put God to the test. And they say this same Alson trades goods in the church, selling her home-made cloth . . .

And they also say the parish priest does not ring the bells at the required times . . .[67]

Before long, a new emphasis in religious art began to be felt. Crucifixions became more lifelike and painful, the sufferings of the Virgin Mary as she watched her son die were more realistically portrayed, and a strange tradition of the *Danse Macabre* appeared, with death as a skeleton, leading the living in an inescapable dance. Suffering, anguish and death were at centre stage in human life, perhaps as never before or since. Life, success and good fortune were transient, and the old answers no longer satisfied. A little later, Dürer produced his great masterpiece of The Four Horsemen of the Apocalypse: War, Famine, Plague and Death, encapsulating the times of trauma and the changes they had forced on his world (plates 17 and 19).

Not surprisingly perhaps, this terrible period led ultimately to new beliefs, and new opportunities for the survivors to forge a different future.

67 W W Capes, ed., *Registrum Johanes Trefnant, Episcopi Herefordensis A.D. 1389-1404* (The Registers of the Bishops of Hereford; Hereford: Canterbury and York Society, 1916), translated by Claire Rush

Chapter 6. New Hope and A New Outlook

The years from the mid 1500s saw a new beginning, a change of direction. Life was not transformed overnight: there were still sporadic attacks of plague, years of poor harvest and hunger, and then the civil wars which saw armies marching through Bromyard itself, but Herefordshire was nevertheless moving into a new future. There were new possibilities, a new outlook, no longer framed by medieval social and personal constraints but offering increased individual opportunities and choice.

As these 'early modern' years pass by, the historical record is able to shine ever more light on the individuals who lived in, owned and shaped Studmarsh. We begin to get to know them as distinct personalities better than we have been able to before. They are no longer merely names, labelled as belonging to the 'servile' 'free' or 'knightly' classes, but real people, with their own unique stories. The archaeological exploration uncovered evidence for their lives, allowing direct contact with their cooking utensils and a chance to stand in the houses where they lived; the historical record provides detailed glimpses of their relationships and hopes for the future. These are the lives that most directly moulded the way Studmarsh is today, and the process of bringing them out of the shadows and into clearer view was a major goal of the project, drawing threads of connection between their past lives and ours. The mirror of mental health recovery reflected the value of the process: individuals emerging from obscurity, respecting common ground, bringing our past in mind to understand the threads of human histories.

New Ways of Being

Out of the trauma and disasters of the fourteenth century, a new community gradually dared to emerge. The survivors became adaptors and innovators, working at new ways of living, just as those adapting to life with a disability are, although few may know it, among the most creative and proactive members of our communities today. With barely half the population, then, there was less pressure to grow grain, and many fields were put down to grass. In Herefordshire, wool production was a popular choice, to be sold to the weaving towns of the Low Countries or, increasingly, to the expanding cloth-manufacturing businesses of Worcester. Leominster wool was famous as some of the finest in England, and the main road past Studmarsh must have been busy with trade and travellers. Fish ponds could also be created easily in the clay soil, while pigs were fed on a rich diet including whey from ewe or cow milk, and even grain which was surplus to human needs. The resulting higher-protein diet was in sharp contrast to what had gone before (plates 20 and 21).

This new and healthier situation led to other changes. Orchards were planted, a small-scale land market developed, and the more enterprising of the emerging breed of yeomen farmers began growing new cash crops as the rural economy expanded. This trend was partly stimulated by the shortages resulting from Henry VIII's wars, when imports were cut off and good profits could be made by growing woad, madder, flax and hemp, for dyes, canvas and rope. Rapeseed was also grown, replacing imported olive oil. The results of experiments with these crops by the new landed gentry quickly filtered down through the social classes, and by the 1650s books and pamphlets were being written in plenty, debating the best way to manage your land or to grow the many new crops being imported from the New World. A major new trend was towards gardening and horticulture, and it came to be realised that even quite small plots of land, if intensively managed, could produce high yields. This was dramatically demonstrated during the famines of the 1590s, when Richard Gardiner of Shrewsbury fed several hundred paupers for three critical 'hungry gap' weeks, largely on carrots he had grown in a field of under four acres. Nothing like this had been achieved before, and this and Gardiner's other work showed conclusively what could be done with new crops and new methods.[68]

The People of Studmarsh

The settlements in Bromyard foreign, decimated by the years of trauma, are described in some detail in Swithin Butterfield's survey, carried out from 1575-1580. Butterfield himself is a shadowy figure; he seems to have been a theologian and mathematician as well as an antiquarian, and apparently was a friend of Bishop John Scory of Hereford.[69] He was able to make use of documents and oral traditions now lost to us, and his description of the local area is as invaluable as it is complicated and unique. One of the most striking things about Butterfield's survey is the evidence for population decline in the preceding years: in both Whitbourne and Bromyard foreign, about half the houses were unoccupied or ruined. Two centuries after their visitations, plague and famine still left their mark. But yet somehow, against the odds, this visibly scarred community was the foundation on which the new Studmarsh was built (plates 22 and 23).

Butterfield's survey is more concerned with land than houses, since it was the land that brought the bishop most of his rents. But even so, we can glean vital clues about the people and their lives. Both Linton and Norton had mills, one on the Linton Brook, south of the main road, another on the Paradise Brook where part of the medieval cruck-framed house still survives. So the people of Studmarsh need not have carried their grain far to have it milled, or to buy flour, and the mills would surely have been ideal places to catch up with the gossip and news from neighbouring hamlets.

There are two houses recorded by Butterfield which may have been in the area now called Studmarsh. In Linton, Richard Biddle had a house called Studmarsh, also known as Yearnes, together with about 15 acres of meadow and pasture. Richard was not actually living there when Butterfield made his notes, but had let it to a man named William Colley. Also in Linton, Hugh Hey held a house called Studcroft, which was let to Widow Bray; it had previously been occupied

68 J Thirsk, *Alternative Agriculture: A History from the Black Death to the Present Day* (Oxford: Oxford University Press, 1997), p. 37
69 A Kneen, 'Who Was Swithin Butterfield?' *Bromyard and District Local History Society Journal* 33 (2011): 11-13

Figure 5: Neighbouring Properties Relating to the Studmarsh Story

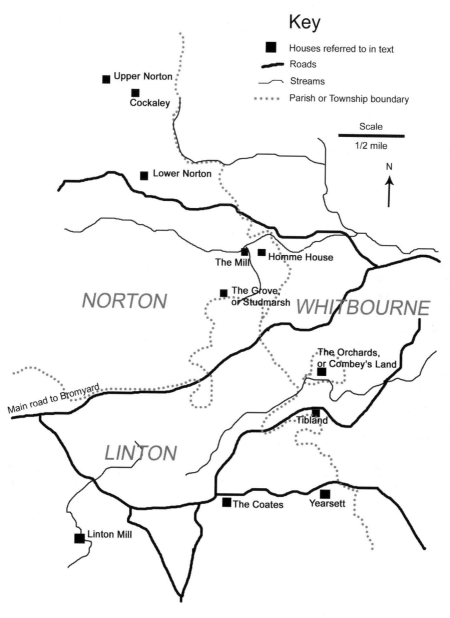

Key

■ Houses referred to in text
— Roads
— Streams
····· Parish or Township boundary

Scale
1/2 mile

N

Upper Norton
Cockaley
Lower Norton
The Mill
Homme House
The Grove, or Studmarsh

NORTON
WHITBOURNE

The Orchards, or Combey's Land

Main road to Bromyard

Tibland

LINTON

The Coates
Yearsett

Linton Mill

by John Arden. It soon became apparent as we explored the archives that the Biddle and Colley families were central to our understanding of the later history of Studmarsh, and Butterfield's survey named several other members of these families. Thus John Colley held two houses and 58 acres around Upper Norton and Cockaley; Richard Colley's widow, Sybil, had a life-interest in a house at Lower Norton, with 90 acres; and a different John Colley held two houses and 59 acres in Winslow. Meanwhile, James Biddle held one house and 30 acres at Combeys Land, by Bringsty Common in Linton. The situation is further confused because there were Biddles, Colleys and Combeys in Whitbourne, who seemed to be related somehow to their Bromyard namesakes.

Without a contemporary map, and without knowing where all the little strips and plots of land were that Butterfield used to explain where he was in the parish, it is impossible to be sure how his survey relates to what we now see in the landscape. Butterfield told us, for example that Walter Oliver's widow Joan had a cottage with six acres of pasture adjacent to the land of Roger Colley and two others, but we could not deduce from this where Widow Oliver lived, nor, as became apparent on closer inspection of Butterfield's text, even if the Roger Colley he was referring to was still alive at the time he was writing. We certainly cannot tell which house Roger Colley lived in, since his fields might have been at some distance from his farmhouse. Also, no parish registers exist before 1538[70] so before this we could not work out detailed family trees, and people's blood relationships eluded us. What we were able to do, as we became more familiar with these people of Tudor Herefordshire, was to begin to understand the friendships and links that made sense of their lives, and so to root them in their communities a little.

The Biddles and Colleys seem to have counted three families among their close neighbours and friends. These were the Bennets and Bromes at Middle Norton, and the Ardens who farmed in Brockhampton and later at Lincetter in Whitbourne. Edmond Brome was himself a relation, having married a Colley in 1546. The strength of the bonds between these families can be glimpsed in the 1560 will of Joan Colley of Whitbourne. One of her two daughters had married John Arden, while the only godchild she named was Walter Biddle. Meanwhile, the earliest will of a Bromyard Colley which we unearthed was that of Roger Colley, who died in 1548 'in old age'. He must have been born many years before Henry VIII came to the throne, and was already an old man before the religious upheavals of the Reformation. Roger served for us as a personal link back to the certainties and also the fears of the medieval past, his will opening a door onto his inner life. In his will, he left four marks (about three months' pay for a skilled labourer) for mending the footpath along the Broad Bridge, the route into Bromyard from the Stourport road. As is the case today, this vital route was liable to flood, and the maintenance of the bridge would have been accepted as a religious duty. Roger's will also shows clearly the intertwining of the small group of families. His executors were his daughter Joan, and William son of the late Philip Colley. The overseers of the will were John Colley and Edmond Brome, while one of the witnesses was James Biddle (plate 22).

The difficulties we face in deciding precisely who was who, how people were related and where they lived is exemplified by another will, that of John Colley of Bromyard, dated 1578 and so right in the middle of the time when Swithun Butterfield was conducting his research. Then, as now, the details of people's lives tend to remain opaque to us, and too much information can obscure the picture rather than clarify it. Like Roger who died thirty years earlier and who might perhaps have been his father, John left a donation for the repair and upkeep of the causeway by Broad Bridge. His beneficiaries included his sister Joan and her family, brother Richard's children including William and Thomas, brother William

---

70 The Whitbourne parish registers only begin in 1585

and his children, another William Colley (described as 'of Badley') and his children, Roger Colley and his son John, Eleanor Arden his goddaughter 'and his other godchildren' and the children of both Edmond Brome and John Arden. Almost as an afterthought, John noted that Thomas, son of his brother Richard, owed him the substantial sum of 100 marks (more than £66) for a property deal in Winslow; this was to be repaid and distributed among his relations. John's executors were to be Roger Colley and John Arden, and among the witnesses were Roger and Robert Bennet and Edmond Brome.

Roger Bennet is one personality who stands out, because he was remarkably long-lived. At the time he witnessed John Colley's will he was already 64, and the burial registers show that he died in Norton in 1620, aged 106. People who survived past childhood ailments and the twin perils of child-birth or, for men, the accidents and dangers of their work, frequently lived into their seventies or even eighties. But to see out a century, a dynasty of monarchs and a radical reshaping of the national psyche, as Roger Bennet did, was rare indeed. He must have been something of a local celebrity and, if he had retained his faculties, a mine of community information.

When we combine the evidence from these and other early wills with the parish records of baptisms, marriages and burials, we can begin to glimpse how the Colley family in the Studmarsh area fitted together. Wills are above all about relationships, families and the friendships that develop in adult life. They are manifestations of the human desire to be remembered, to have had a worthwhile and connected life. The Roger who died in 1548 may have been the father of some of the other Colleys named, although we do not have baptism records far enough back to prove it. Similarly, there is a will of a Thomas Colley, dated 1552, which tells us that he had a brother called Robert, and his wife was called Katherine. We could not place these people in the family tree, but we know Katherine was left with two young children, a daughter and five year old William, when Thomas died.

In the next generation of the Colley family, there was the John who died in 1578; he was childless, but as we have seen above, his surviving siblings were Joan, William and Richard, all of whom had families. With this Richard Colley, brother of John, we are suddenly on firmer ground, because we have more documents to guide us. We know that he married Sybil Pharington in 1547, and they had eight children before Richard died in 1571. Nine months later, Sybil married Robert Bennet, presumably the same person who later witnessed John Colley's will. People were very thin on the ground and had to rely on each other, forming a close-knit community whether they liked it or not! Of Richard and Sybil's children, two are of particular interest for the history of Studmarsh: their eldest two sons Thomas, born in 1550, who was the one who had borrowed heavily from his uncle John, and William, born 1552. This William married in 1588, the year of the Spanish Armada when beacons were lit right across the country; several would have been visible from near Studmarsh, as the warning spread north.

Despite all this detailed evidence, which we analysed carefully and tried hard to make sense of, we still have no idea which William Colley was renting Studmarsh House from Richard Biddle in the mid-1570s. There seems to be no way of solving

Figure 6: The Colley Family Tree

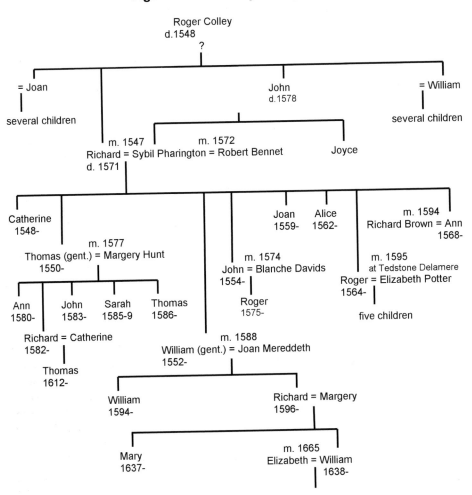

this mystery. Was it Richard's son William, aged 25 or so, still single but having perhaps moved out of the family home as his siblings grew up? Or was it one of his cousins: William son of Thomas, five years older than him, or the even older William, son of Philip, overseer of Roger Colley's will of 1548? Or just possibly it was a son of William Colley of Badley Wood in Whitbourne.

The ownership of Studmarsh at the time of Butterfield's survey is slightly clearer. There are other surviving documents which show that the man called James Biddle who is recorded as owning Combeys and Studmarsh House in Linton, was quite wealthy. He also had property in Whitbourne (five farms including Huntlands, Pittclose and the present Old Gaines), and further afield the manor of Hatfield, west of Bromyard, and land in Suckley, Worcestershire. But he died in 1576, so in the Whitbourne survey (conducted there in 1577) Butterfield noted that James' widow Joan was already remarried and her second husband held two of her Whitbourne farms. In Bromyard, however, Butterfield's survey spanned several years; James Biddle is one of the people who died while the work was in progress, and he is described as still owning his land. James' brother Richard was living at either Combeys or Studmarsh when James died, while James and Joan were themselves based in Hatfield. It is not known when they were married, or even when James was born, but they only seem to have had two surviving daughters.

James Biddle's will has survived, and the scale of his legacies give some indication of his wealth: 20 gold coins called nobles to each of his sister's seven children, £20 to each of his two daughters, his brother William and a resident of Bromyard, and over a pound to each of seven servants, with lesser sums to two other servants. The only family member who seems to have done rather badly was his brother Robert, who was bequeathed James' favourite three-year-old cow! Meanwhile, James took great care providing for his orphaned niece, whose parents had both died in the last six years. Predictably, perhaps, the Colley family are also mentioned in this will, but again it is not clear which individuals they are. James gave £2 to each of the three daughters of William Colley, to be held in trust until the time of their marriage, which suggests they were still only young. Was this the William Colley who had been renting Studmarsh House, and may still have been living there? Or was it a Whitbourne Colley who was perhaps a friend and near neighbour? We know that a William Colley owned a house near Sapey Bridge, barely a mile from Gaines, so perhaps this was the person concerned (plates 24 and 25).

As with Richard and Sybil Colley, it is when we come to James' brother Richard that we can be more confident of the outlines of individual lives, even if the detail is still hazy. When he inherited Studmarsh House from his brother James, Richard had only been married for seven years, to Margery Bennet (presumably a relation of Roger and Robert). Either he married late or, since his brother James only had two children, perhaps both Richard and James were relatively young when James died. Either theory could fit with what we know of their sister: if she was the oldest in the family and had married young (perhaps at eighteen), she would only need to have been in her early thirties to have seven surviving children. Even this may be an over-estimate, since as we shall see twins ran in the family. We do know that Richard and Margery Biddle went on to have seven children, two of whom, both called James, died in infancy.

It is sometimes asked whether parents grieved for their children as much then, when it was so common to bury one or more as infants. There is little enough firm evidence, but making the effort to carry a sickly newborn baby all the way into Bromyard from the edge of the common, only to retrace the route two days later for its burial, as Richard Biddle did, must surely have been a heart-rending journey. Especially would this be so since he was their first child, with the particular emotional investment that entails. It has been suggested that choosing the same name for a younger son could show a lack of attachment to the memory of the first, lost, child, but it could equally reflect a desire for the memories to live on, or merely a strong family attachment to the name, in this case James.

It was Richard and Margery's younger son, Roger, one of the twins born in 1575, who probably later inherited Studmarsh House. Richard himself died in 1584, and his widow remarried the next year, to a man with the improbable name of Florence Stephens (alias Symons). It was quite usual to remarry quickly when there was a

Figure 7: The Early Part of the Biddle Family Tree

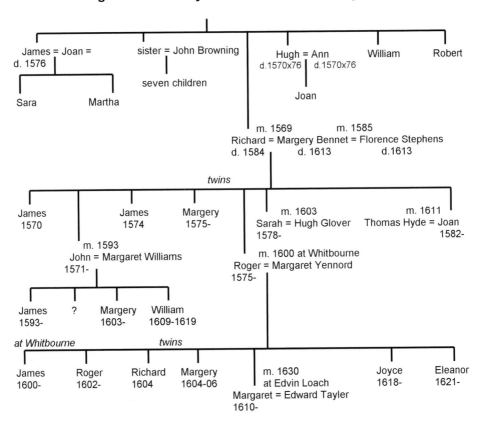

family of young children to care for, especially for yeomen who needed both men and women to run a successful farm. Margery and Florence lived until 1613, when they died within a few months of each other.

So much for Studmarsh House. What of the other house, called Studcroft, which Butterfield said was owned by Hugh Hey, and had been let successively to John Arden and Widow Bray? It seems from the point in the text where Butterfield described it that this house may have been somewhere in the north of Linton, within half a mile of Studmarsh, but more than this we cannot say. Hugh Hey himself was for some reason living in one of the houses at Yearsett at the time, as a tenant. The only plausible will for this Hugh Hey that survives is dated 1599, and it only mentions land in Suckley, Worcestershire, with a request that Hugh should be buried in Bockleton, north-west of Bromyard. The pattern of Hey's land ownership is intriguingly similar to that of James Biddle, but without any further clues this line of research had to be abandoned. Nor is there a burial or a remarriage for Widow Bray in Bromyard or nearby, which might have helped us to understand events more clearly. As with the test pits, these promising investigations came to nothing. One odd thing about Butterfield's account is that both these houses, Studcroft and Studmarsh, were listed in Linton, while the evidence on the ground says that part of the old Studmarsh settlement was in Norton. Without other discoveries to guide us further, however, we should perhaps accept for now that both these houses are likely to have been somewhere in what we now think of as Studmarsh. The question is, where?

There are three obvious candidates for the sites of the last two surviving houses of Studmarsh, if these are the two referred to by Butterfield. Firstly, the house excavated in Trench 1, which current evidence suggests was abandoned by about 1550 or soon after, although we have no closer reliable dating. Secondly, there is the now-abandoned cottage and garden on the edge of the site, which is known to have been occupied into the twentieth century; unfortunately, without any exploratory work on the site we cannot draw even tentative conclusions about when it was first in use. Thirdly, there is the still-occupied house known as The Grove or Grove Farm, on the north-west corner of the site. Of these, the first is clearly in Norton, while the other two are close to the township boundary, one on each side.

In the absence of any information about the recently-abandoned cottage, the best we can do is to cast the net wider, and follow up what is found. But, to continue the analogy of fishing, no amount of trawling through archives identified any further reference to Studcroft. After Butterfield mentions that Widow Bray was living in it in about 1575, it seems to vanish. Can we perhaps imagine that Hugh Hey, who had other property nearby in Linton, did not wish to live at Studcroft? Under the medieval hierarchy of tenants it was originally classified as a free holding, superior to the customary holding of Studmarsh House; but what if the building itself had become a less desirable home as others were modernised and extended? If this were true, and especially if the cottage by the hollow way were not yet built, then one could imagine Widow Bray spending her last years as a tenant here in the property whose foundations were uncovered in our trench, before it was finally allowed to fall into ruin after her death.

For this theory to be workable, we needed clear evidence for either The Grove or the cottage on the edge of the common being the house that James Biddle called Studmarsh. To search for this evidence, we looked further into the Biddle family history, delving down into the traces of their lives that they have left behind. Of course, it is impossible to be sure of precise relationships and so any family tree we construct will be only an informed guess. It is often difficult today to unpick the complexities of family life, and at a distance of over 300 years the problems are far worse. We face several particular challenges with the Biddle family at Bromyard. A very large proportion of Biddle babies were baptised with the same few names, so that for instance in the hundred years after 1570, half the males were either called James or Richard, while a third of the females were Margaret. Also, there was no obligation to have burials or christenings in the parish where you were resident, and weddings were traditionally held in the bride's parish, so tracing a particular individual is very difficult. And in any case, the parish records are not complete, even in a parish like Bromyard where they are better than many. As many as ten or twenty percent of all baptisms, burials and even marriages may not have been copied into the registers, and during the Civil War and Commonwealth, 1642-1660, when the Church of England was compromised, the Bromyard registers are almost blank.

What we do know with reasonable certainty is that Richard and Margery Biddle had two surviving sons, John and Roger, both of whom married women called Margaret. Both in turn christened their eldest son James, but there the similarities end. The elder, John, may have left the Bromyard area, since no unequivocal later evidence for him, his wife or children was found in the locality. The younger, Roger, married Margaret Yennord of Whitbourne in 1600, when he was twenty-five. Roger was born in the year before his uncle James died, so if his parents moved to Studmarsh when they inherited it, he would have been the first Biddle to grow up there, knowing only Studmarsh House as home. Roger and Margaret were also the first generation in England not to have lived through the turmoil of the Reformation, with the dissolution of the monasteries and the destruction almost overnight of the system of social care, refuges and schools that the monastic houses offered. The Reformation also swept away and outlawed the whole calendar of social events which bound late medieval communities together, the culture that gave the year shape and meaning: the patronal festival for St Peter's Church on 29th June, summer bonfires for St John after harvest, feasting for Michaelmas and All Saints, fasting in Advent, when fish not meat was on the menu, the twelve glorious days of Christmas to balance the solemn time of Lent and Holy Week, before the year began again at Easter, with processions and public games.

But the Reformation was not destined to be a simple progression into a new world order. No sooner was the new Protestant faith in place, than the Catholic Queen Mary took over from her brother Edward, and reversed all the changes. Now suddenly everything had to be put back, on pain of terrible punishment. Candles reappeared on altars, new statues of saints were made, or the old ones hastily retrieved from their resting places, confession was once more required, the old prayers were heard again and old beliefs promoted. Then, after five short years of confusion, Mary died and was succeeded by her protestant but pragmatic sister, Queen Elizabeth. England was finally allowed to take slow steps towards religious toleration.

Roger and Margaret Biddle must have heard many stories about these chaotic times, as they and their siblings grew up, times when it was impossible to know what to believe and where to turn for spiritual help. For them, though, it probably felt like an age long gone. By the time they were married in 1600, Elizabeth I had been on the throne for over forty years, and the New World was just over the horizon. Their first child, James, was baptised at Whitbourne, the new mother's home parish, suggesting that Margaret was close to her own mother and wanted to be with her at this challenging time in her life. In all, Roger and Margaret had seven children, like his parents had done, including twins who both died young. After this, however, we suddenly come up against one of those periods for which the evidence is only patchy at best, when it is hard to make a coherent story. It may be that their son Roger inherited Studmarsh, and he may have had two sons, Roger and Richard, but little is known for certain because this was a time when the Bromyard parish records were poorly kept. Some taxation records help us out at the end of this thin time, showing that both Roger and Richard Biddle had houses in Linton in the 1660s, and Richard's was significantly grander, with two chimneys.[71]

The next firm evidence for Studmarsh also concerns a Richard Biddle, presumably this same man with the two-hearthed house. He died in 1674 and was probably the great-grandson of the Richard who had inherited it from his brother James a hundred years earlier. We cannot tell exactly when Richard was born, but it would have been about 1625. Nor do we know when or where he married, since this was during the upheavals of the Civil War, when parish church records were seldom kept. We do however know that his wife was called Mary, while his will reveals that they had at least five children: four daughters and a son, also called Richard.[72] The two youngest daughters, Elizabeth and Abigail, were born in 1657 and 1663, the one shortly before Oliver Cromwell died and the other after the Restoration of King Charles II.

Figure 8: The Later Part of the Biddle Family Tree

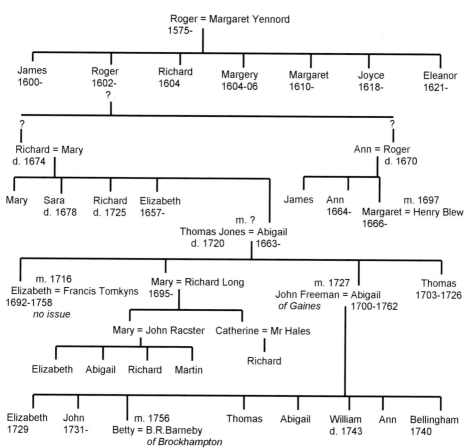

71 Hearth Tax, Linton, 1664, 1671, BDLHS E179/119/492 and E179/248/14
72 HRO probate registers

The survival of Richard Biddle's will is a little miracle. It is a treasure-trove of information about his family, his ambitions for his land, his care and hopes for his family, and even the detail of his house contents. More than the earlier Colley family wills, it helps us to relate to Richard as a person, despite the passage of three centuries (plates 26 and 27). It begins in a conventional way, although he does not mention King Charles in the preamble, which may be local convention, or it may possibly suggest a residue of Puritanism. Certainly, he goes to considerable lengths to proclaim his firm belief in the Protestant view of redemption. As with the hearth tax listing mentioned above, he says he is 'of Linton in the parish of Bromyard', not of Norton. The main section of his will is worth transcribing in full:

> . . . Item, I give and bequeath unto my two eldest daughters Mary Beedle
> and Sara Beedle one meadow called by the name of Studmarsh
> for and during their two natural lives and the life of the longest
> liver of them after the decesse of Mary my wife and if that they
> doe break up any parte of it to the use of a hoppiard I doe give them
> the coppie at Norchard lying by the brook side to manner it with
> poules. Item I give and bequeath unto Elizabeth Beedle my third daughter
> the sum of £30 to be paid when she shall accomplish the
> age of one and twenty years or upon the day of her marriage. Likewise I
> give and bequeath unto Abigail Beedle my youngest daughter the sum
> of £30 to be paid when shee shall accomplish the age of
> one and twenty years or upon the day of her marriage. Likewise I
> give and bequeath unto my son and heir Richard Beedle the table boards and
> frame in the hall and the bedd steads in the chamber. Item I give and
> bequeath unto Mary Beedle my wife all my free land during her naturall
> life. Likewise I give and bequeath unto Mary Beedle my
> wife all the rest of my goods cattell and chattels corne and graine
> after my decese, my debts and funeral expenses being paid, whome
> I doe make my full and whole executrix of this my last will and testament
> . . .

Richard's will also includes an inventory of all his valuables, recorded three days after his burial. (One of the valuers was, incidentally, an Edward Colley, who probably farmed at Brockhampton at this time and also had connections in Whitbourne, where he was buried in 1680. This was the last evidence we found for a link between the two families, and so the Colleys pass out of the Studmarsh story and into Norton, where they continued to live.) As with the will, this inventory of Richard's possessions sheds intimate light on his daily life:

> An Inventorie of all the goodes and chattels late of Richard Beedle of Linton . . .

	li.	s.	d.
Imprimis, his wearing Apparrell	1	6	8
Item, in the hall one Table bord and frame			
two chairs one forme one Joyne cubord	0	13	4
Lining of all sortes	3	0	0

Item two fether Bedd steads and three coffers	1	0	0
Item four Blankets one Coverlete two thrum cloths	1	0	0
Brass and Pewter of all sortes	2	0	0 . . .

And among his farming equipment is recorded:

Item hodgsheds and other coupery ware	1	0	0
Item one Cider mill	0	16	0
Item three Acres of Rye	2	10	0
Item fower Acres of Lent graine	1	6	8
Item Hay	1	10	0
Item three bullocks	6	0	0
Item two kine	4	5	0
Item two yeare old beste and two calves	3	0	0
Item one old mare	1	10	0
Item thre Yewes and Lames	0	15	0
Item: Implements of husbandry of all sortes and other lumber forgotten	0	10	0

The Total is   £35 7s 8d

No neighbours or friends were included in Richard's bequests, but this may simply be because he was leaving three dependent children and needed to provide for them. He was clearly not a poor man, since he was able to leave £60 for his younger daughters' dowries. The bedroom furnishings were also relatively expensive, with superior feather beds not cheaper flock ones, and the brass and pewter tableware indicates a generally prosperous household. As well as these plates, dishes and perhaps candlesticks, it would be reasonable to assume that Richard and Mary had some pottery for daily use, probably of the black or yellow-combed types found in Test Pits 2 and 3 (plate 28).

It is when we look at Richard Biddle's farming concerns that we meet him personally. The inventory shows that it was a mixed farm, with livestock, arable and at least one orchard. The combination of cider press and barrels leaves little room for doubt that he was making his own cider, as many Herefordshire yeomen did. It would have been given to those helping him with haymaking and harvest, and consumed by the family through the year as long as it lasted. He was growing a mix of rye and wheat, hedging his bets with the weather; these crops in the fields must have been just ripe for harvest when the inventory was taken at the end of July, making them much easier to value. The hay would be the first cut, already stored in the barn for use in the coming winter: the high value of his three bullocks and two cows (kine) shows clearly the necessity for a good stock of hay. By contrast, it is apparent that Richard was not specialising in wool-growing, but only keeping a few ewes for domestic use. Touchingly, he had kept his old mare long beyond her prime, presumably to save the walk into Bromyard to market and church; had he anticipated eventually replacing her with a younger horse from a neighbour rather than breeding from her in her old age?

As well as embracing the modern way of farming, Richard Biddle seems to have been keen to look forward and try new things. It may well be that he had been planning to plant hops on part of Studmarsh meadow when he was taken ill; certainly he had thought through the implications of how much wood would be needed for the poles. Rather than give his elder two daughters cash dowries, he chose to give them the meadow, with a strong inducement to try this new crop which, after earlier beginnings in the south-east of England had become a craze which reached Worcestershire and Herefordshire in the years before Richard made his will. It would be a challenge and a risk: not every hopyard was a success, and some years were very poor. But with a good harvest, small fortunes could be made in a single year: with care and hard work, the risks were worth taking. Pamphlets were written and circulated on the best way to grow hops to meet the new taste for beer, and it was generally agreed that two or three acres was all that could be managed on a one-man farm. Even so, with skilful drying this was enough to make an enterprising farmer rich. Two acres of hops could make as much profit as fifty acres of arable. The best advice at this time was that hops should be grown on small, well-manured hills, which had to be dug by hand, with poles set into these and the plants then trained up them.[73] This style of land use might well explain the mysterious checker-board patterns in the grass at Studmarsh. There is no absolute proof that Mary and Sarah did plant part of the meadow with hops, but it is probable that they did; apart from the encouragement they were given and the curious features in part of the meadow (plate 1), the land at Orchards, which is a strong candidate for being 'Narchards', did remain joined to Studmarsh for some years, as we were later able to show.

As so often seems to be the case, however, we soon came up against another missing link in this story. We know that Richard's widow Mary took possession of a house called Stud Marsh in 1674 on behalf of their son Richard, who was presumably still a minor. The second daughter, Sarah, died four years later, leaving the oldest, Mary, to manage the hopyard if they had developed it. We also discovered that Richard junior died in 1725, leaving no heirs. The youngest daughter, Abigail, meanwhile, married the wealthy Thomas Jones of Whitbourne. But we do not know when or where Abigail and Thomas married. The most likely explanation for this is that the wedding was at the chapel at Brockhampton, either the old one down by Lower Brockhampton House, or perhaps in one where the present chapel was later constructed, up by Brockhampton Mansion: there is some evidence which suggests that there may have been an intermediate phase of building at this site.[74]

If Abigail Biddle and Thomas Jones were married at Brockhampton, we have no proof of it, no evidence for when the wedding took place, and it is unlikely that we could ever find out any more about it. Whereas all the parish register books for Bromyard survive from their beginning in 1538 (even though there are gaps in the entries), at least two volumes of the Brockhampton registers are now missing, so they only cover the years from 1757 to 1812. In a strange way Abigail, and her descendants who shared her unusual name, became symbolic for us of the difficulties of understanding the lives of people in the past. She became an emblem of the hidden-ness, the sometimes deliberately disguised depths of other

---

73 Thirsk, *Alternative Agriculture*, pp. 96-103
74 see the 1727 will of Isabella Barnaby, who requests burial with her husband, 83 years before the present chapel where they are interred was built: HRO probate registers; BDLHS Cc. C91/22/41

people's lives, both past and present. The more places we searched, the harder we tried, the more elusive she seemed to become, even though we did discover a great deal about her family. For those of us working on the history of Studmarsh, she became a running theme reminding us that all lives are in some sense 'other', not just the lives of those who lived centuries ago.

In contrast to the mystery surrounding their wedding, Abigail and Thomas' later life is revealed in some detail in his will, which dates to 1720:[75]

> I Thomas Jones of the Orchards in the parish of Bromyard . . . Gent.
> . . . give and bequeath unto my daughter Elizabeth Tomkins the sum of fifty pounds. Item I give to my said daughter Elizabeth the use of the sum of two hundred pounds for her life and after her decease I give the said two hundred pounds to her child or children equally . . .
> . . . if she happen to die without issue which said sum I then give to the child or children of my daughter Mary Long if she hath any then living . . .
> . . . Item I give to my said daughter Mary Long fifty pounds. Item I give to my daughter Mary the use of two hundred pounds for her life . . .
> . . . Item I give and bequeath unto my daughter Abigail the sum of one thousand pounds my best chest of drawers and the bedd over the hall. Item I give to the three children of my sister Margaret Ward ten pounds apiece to be paid to them when they shall severally attain the age of sixteen. Item I give and bequeath all the rest of my household goods . . .
> to my son Thomas when he shall come to the age of one and twenty. Item I give devise and bequeath all the rents fines and profits of all my messuages lands tenements and premises whatsoever unto my said daughter Abigail and son Thomas to be equally divided between them till my said son Thomas shall come to the age of one and twenty. Item I give devise and bequeath all my freehold messuages lands tenements and hereditaments whatsoever to my said son Thomas Jones his heirs and assigns forever . . .
> . . . but if my said son Thomas shall happen to depart this life before the time of the attainment of the age of one and twenty years without issue then I give devise and bequeath all my said freehold . . .
> to my said two daughters Mary and Abigail . . .
> . . . Item I give and bequeath all the rest . . . of my . . . personall estate . . . not herein before disposed of to my said daughter Abigail and son Thomas to be equally divided between them share and share alike and I do hereby make . . . my said daughter Abigail and son Thomas joint executors . . .

75 Public Record Office: CCC Probate 11/580, 171-172

Abigail and Thomas Jones' eldest daughter, Elizabeth, married Francis Tomkyns of Stretton Grandison, but as her father seems to have feared when he made his will, they had no children. After Francis died, Elizabeth moved back to live at The Orchards. The next daughter, Mary, also married and one of her grandchildren was called Abigail. The two younger children, Abigail and Thomas, were very generously provided for. In the event, Thomas junior died unmarried aged 23, leaving his sister Abigail with most of the family's wealth. Why she was so well provided for adds further to the aura of mystery which surrounds her name. When she was 27, this Abigail married John Freeman, the heir to the Gaines estate in Whitbourne, which in a nice closing of the circle included several houses which had once been owned by her ancestor James Biddle. Abigail and John had eight children, including yet another Abigail.

Richard Biddle junior meanwhile continued to live at Studmarsh House with his widowed mother Mary, and remained there after her death. There is no evidence for him ever marrying or having children. The Bromyard manor records show that his mother was certainly still there with him in 1690, and it is possible that she is the Mary Biddle who died in October 1713. If so, she would have been about 85 years old and would have been a widow for 39 years.

This Richard Biddle junior died in 1725 and the following year his eldest niece, Elizabeth Tomkyns, inherited three houses from him. Her will, written in 1753, names these properties as The Coates at Linley Green with three acres, Tibland (further east along Linley Lane) with seven acres, and Studmarsh 'otherwise called The Grove', with a ten acre meadow. Here then, at last, is as good a proof as we could wish for that the house now known as The Grove, and the meadow where the excavations took place, is one and the same place as the Studmarsh which Richard Biddle inherited from his brother James back in 1574. Studmarsh and The Orchards both appear to have been owned by young Abigail at the time of her marriage to John Freeman soon afterwards.

Elizabeth Tomkyns' will shows that by the end of her life she was a very wealthy lady by Bromyard standards. She gave her sister Abigail forty pounds just to buy her mourning clothes, and ten pounds each to Abigail's husband John Freeman and their five surviving children, also for mourning. Her numerous properties were divided up between her relatives, with Studmarsh and its meadow again going to her sister Abigail. In a careful codicil to her will, Elizabeth allocated her most treasured possessions. It is an equally revealing document as the inventory for her grandfather Richard's farm at Studmarsh, but shows how far the family, and society generally, had moved on in material terms. One great nephew was left six parlour chairs, a fire shovel, tongs and fender; her sister Abigail received her best grey negligée, a black damask quilted petticoat, her best stays, the choice of eight shifts, a velvet cloak and her best mourning dress; young Abigail Freeman at Gaines was given a round mahogany table and a corner cupboard; Betty Freeman, a square mahogany table and a chest of drawers with a mirror.

A few months after Elizabeth wrote this codicil, her sister Abigail's daughter Betty married Bartholomew Richard Barneby of Brockhampton, thereby linking the two biggest estates in the neighbourhood and transferring Studmarsh to Brockhampton.

It was Betty and Bartholomew who began transforming the Brockhampton estate, building the new Mansion and landscaping the parkland. In this way, the history of Studmarsh seemed complete, with its ownership traced from Tudor times to today, and with good evidence that the house now called The Grove is the same site that James Biddle left to his brother Richard in 1576.

A Post Script or a Foreword?

While investigating the story of Studmarsh, we uncovered the lives of many people from the past. Some, like Widow Bray, remain shadowy figures, while others we have got to know in more depth. Many of the avenues we tried to follow up turned out to be dead ends and had to be abandoned, either because the trail went cold or because we ran out of time. Overall, it was certainly a far better result than we could have dared to hope for, and the gaps and failures were only to be expected. What we did not anticipate was that the archives would reveal one last surprise, kept hidden until the very last minute.

The text of this book was already part-written when two members of the research team decided to have a look at one last will, simply because it was listed as having two Biddles as beneficiaries. The temptation to carry on exploring and delving into the past, long after the time had run out, was just too great. In the event, this will did not change the results of the project in any fundamental way, but it did shed an unexpected light on one of the central characters, and so pointed up the importance of never assuming that the story is fully told. It filled in a gap that we hadn't even realised was there.

Hugh Wyn of Whitbourne, whose will of 1559/60 supplied this additional insight, was far richer than most men of his acquaintance. His debts when he died amounted to £44, but his inventory totalled £116. As well as this ready money, Hugh had four farms, which he named as Dylwyns, Pitthouse, Gaines and Huntlands. But Hugh only had two children, both of whom were minors, and he was obviously not confident they would survive to inherit his land. Hugh appointed James Biddle, who he described as 'my especiall trustie ffriend and kinsman' as his sole executor and also the children's guardian and tutor; he was selected for this task ahead of Hugh's brother-in-law, who is only described as 'my trustie friend'. James was given the use of the farms and asked to use the rent-income to pay for bringing up the children, and if either should die before adulthood, the money was to go to the other one (plates 30 and 31).

Although it would have made a more exciting story, there was no reason we could see to suppose that James was unworthy of Hugh's trust. It also seemed probable that he was the same James Biddle who we met earlier, when he left Studmarsh to his brother Richard. Indeed, Hugh mentions a Robert Biddle in his will, who could be James and Richard's brother of that name. These were, however, the years of the population crisis, with many unexpected deaths and abnormally high mortality. How James was related to Hugh Wyn, and why he was trusted so much more than the brother-in-law, we may never know. It does however seem that both the children died young. Hugh's last word on the farms was that if this happened,

James was to 'dispose of it all as he shall thincke good'. At the time of James' death in 1576, we already know that he held Gaines, Huntlands and 'Pittclose' farms, so presumably what he had 'thought good' was to keep them in his own hands for the time being.

So we end the story of Studmarsh with a modification to the version of events we thought we had uncovered. It seems that James Biddle had held the bulk of his lands in Whitbourne for less than sixteen years. They were not his ancestral place, the home of his childhood, after all, but had come to him through his 'trustie friendship' for a fellow farmer when they were living through difficult times together.

Chapter 7. A Day in the Life of Past in Mind

What is the legacy of Past in Mind? Was it a small heritage project, which made some discoveries about one little meadow in Herefordshire? Was it a challenging but ultimately successful inter-disciplinary piece of research? Or was it a prototype for something more far-reaching, an attempt to explore the very nature of collaborative work across a wide range of subjects? Did it succeed in combining historical research with 'positively placing past in mind'?

To find the answer to these questions requires both a look back to the basis on which the project was set up, and a look forward to the way its conclusion was celebrated.

Foundations

Research in the arts, humanities and social sciences is often constrained by the assumptions, limitations and 'world view' of the project design or the individual worker. In this respect, Past in Mind had an advantage from the start. As explained in Chapter One, it was designed to function across three disciplines, each with their own sub-texts of diversity and tension. As a result, a fundamental feature of it was the care that had gone into the support of participants, allowing opportunities for bridge-building and interaction as the research story developed. As project historian, I brought my own interests and preconceptions of what makes for 'good research'; much of this was based on sound method-training, but some was undoubtedly my personal slant and not necessarily useful for the project. At times, I was helped to acknowledge the value of different perspectives for this project, by the framework itself. The archaeologists had to manage an intensive excavation period using a volunteer community workforce, with additional difficulties imposed by a summer which must have been one of the wettest since 1317 and an inaccessible and poorly-drained site. Meanwhile, all those of us who were unfamiliar with the concepts and realities of the mental health recovery model had a great deal to learn.

Was Past in Mind a small heritage project, which made some discoveries about one little meadow in Herefordshire? Yes, it was, and it delivered a detailed and rich story, in a critically under-researched county. It was an example of good practice which has the potential to act as a model for understanding other communities in the county. Was Past in Mind a challenging but ultimately successful inter-disciplinary piece of research? Yes, it was, but the challenges and pitfalls were assessed in advance and safety mechanisms were already in place. It was not without its problems, but it delivered in all its target areas. It demonstrated that if and when those with expertise of whatever sort (academic, practical or personal experience) find ways of co-operating, the whole is much greater than the sum of the parts. Was Past in Mind in fact a prototype for an exploration of the very nature of collaborative work across a wide range of subjects? Again, I would say yes, because it was not 'just a token occupational therapy task'. It was not just a way of getting heritage research done on the cheap by using free labour. It was not just about bridge-building between mental health service users and the wider community. Instead, the research became a shared journey of discovery. The common underlying methodologies involved in mental health recovery, archaeology and local social history enriched the discoveries and progress made across the board; the worst century in recorded history was brought to life through the insights of modern project participants in the torrential rain of 2012, and the common humanity of the people of Studmarsh Past shed unexpected light on today.

And Celebration

Among the more distinctive features of Past in Mind was that it was not concluded with a seminar, or a series of research papers, or even an exhibition, although all these things have played their part. Instead, the grand finale of the project was a celebration, entitled 'A Day in the Life.' It was felt that people, particular people in the past as well as the lives of participants both now and earlier in their own personal journeys, were so fundamental to its nature, that Past in Mind could only end with a celebration of these people and their lives. As much as anything, it helped to acknowledge that the journeys of discovery, both personal and about the history of the site and other settlements like it, were not over.

A Day in the Life featured vignettes drawn from the Studmarsh discoveries, written by the project participants. Most were performed in period costume, and for many this was an important opportunity to become further immersed in the role. For some who elected to take part, participation itself was deeply cathartic.

Past in Mind was a truly eclectic gathering. Nobody wore labels, and pre-judgements usually turned out to be quite wrong, as this **Day in the Life of a Student on Past in Mind** shows.

I am a student
I come in many forms -
I am the archaeology undergraduate on fieldwork practice
I am the sixth former not yet decided
I am her friend from an African conflict where education stopped
I am Benjamin, in my third year of a nursing degree
I am all of these and more, and I am now a volunteer in Studmarsh excavating the past!
What did I expect? I didn't know.
Should I be here? I have no experience of surveying or excavating!
Should I be here with people from Mind? I didn't know.
Who is a volunteer and who is not? Who is an archaeologist and who is not?
Who has mental health problems and who has not?
When you look at me, the student, what do you see? Do I wear a hoodie and do drugs?
You're not sure?
Do you know I'm shy and want to find my way in the world?

Will I be accepted on this dig? Will I feel different? Will I stand out? How will I know what to do? What will I learn?

This is what I learned –
We were <u>all</u> nervous and unsure and excited and a little lost. And eager to gain knowledge and skills. And we all had fun and shared jokes with Chris and Dai and with each other. We found pottery and uncovered walls and felt just a little in touch with the young and the old, the women and the men from all those years ago, and with each other as volunteers. We all became students of discovery at this place called Studmarsh.

One member of the project group grew up at Studmarsh, and for her the research triggered questions of childhoods long gone, in **A Day in the Life of a Real Child of Studmarsh.**

My memories of Studmarsh go back to the hot summer of 1976, when the spring in Bond's Dingle was the ideal place for cooling off in the hot summer sun. It set me wondering if the Biddle and Colley children of Studmarsh and Studcroft used it during the hot summers of the 1570s. Four hundred years had passed, had this place really changed that much in that time?

Just a few years after the Battle of Worcester, Elizabeth Biddle was born in 1657 and sister Abigail in 1663, the youngest of a large family, and may well have played in that same spring at Bond's Dingle as teenagers. Their parents Richard and Mary, just like my own, didn't have to worry that they would come to any harm but would return home as soon as they were tired and hungry.

Fifty years before them, Plague had caused twenty-four deaths in the Bromyard area.

During the harsh winter of 1977/78 we sledged down Studmarsh bank on empty fertilisers bags. I wonder what the Colley children would have used as sledges four hundred years previously when in 1577 there is an alliance between England and the Netherlands and Francis Drake sails around the world. I'd like to think that their father William would have made them a makeshift sledge!
Did they let the Biddle children, John and the toddlers Roger and Margaret, join in their fun?

Annoyingly for myself and my siblings, school got in the way of these activities; however this was not the case for the children of Studmarsh and Studcroft all those years ago. The girls would have been raised to marry well and the boys educated at home in book-keeping and farm business.

I suppose we will never know for sure whether we played the same on Studmarsh but I'm sure that we would all agree on one thing, be it four or five hundred years ago or just yesterday, Studmarsh was the ideal place to grow up.

Past in Mind began with two history research training days, the second of which included a visit to the County Record Office. Lots of ground was covered, but it turned out that it was the seriousness of the project's aims that made the greatest impression on many, as this **Day in the Life of a Volunteer in 'The Volley'** describes.

I have just entered The Volunteer Inn, Harold Street, in Hereford. Brimming with people, bursting with chatter its strong current sweeps me inside – I almost feel as if I am drowning.

Sitting in the back room of the aptly named Volunteer Inn are a sizeable group of volunteers. There is tangible excitement and expectancy. We are beginning our research today. No one knows where this might take us. I am already captivated by the idea of exploring uncharted territory. The sense of adventure helps me to overcome the claustrophobia which is starting to smother me in this crowded room.

Good research techniques are vital, and I eagerly digest the information being given to us. I can feel the dust that has gathered since my University days. It forms a furry film across my grey matter, and I have an overwhelming urge to shake my head in order to disperse it.

But the old thrill of those bookworm days comes leaping back as I realise that this project is seriously academic. We are visiting the Records Office in a minute, and I am carried away by a wave of childish excitement at the thought. Then my stomach drops as anxiety gnaws away inside me. I might not be up for this. My brain could have eroded from twenty years of rust for all I know. At least I am not short of enthusiasm, and this eases my apprehension.

Once in the Records Office the enormity of the Past in Mind Project hits me. This Victorian building is stuffed with ancient maps and manuscripts dating back centuries. Everyone in here right now is a mere pin point on the landscape of time. I wonder if anyone will come across my name in a few centuries from now, when I am but an archive. It makes me realise just how mortal we all are.

I feel privileged to be a volunteer. This is giving me the chance to make a genuine contribution – to the National Archive, to the local community, to our group. I am spurred on by this thought, and I know that the other volunteers are driven in a similar way. I cannot help feeling exhilarated and optimistic. This feels really, really good.

The archaeological excavation focussed on the areas of the site which might provide evidence about the period when Studmarsh's population shrank. The historical work confirmed that this took place in the centuries of plague and famine in the later middle ages. The pivotal event was the Black Death, and the traumas people lived through then drew profound insights from the project participants, as these next two cameos show.

A Day in the Life of The Black Death.

I am the Black Death. I hover near a labourer's sick bed and embrace the physician who tends the dying man. I breathe over the Vicar as he hurries in with oil and prayer book. I tiptoe round the maidens who are weeping outside, and two of them I kiss. And finally I whisper into grandfather's ear that I shall see him tomorrow. My work is done at this small cottage in Studmarsh.

Sweeping my black cloak along the grass I stride onwards towards the mighty house of stone. I am the Black Death. I do not discriminate. Rich or poor, strong or infirm, rosy wench or fair-haired lad – I see no difference between them. Thus half the population of Studmarsh I carry off to the graveyard. And half I leave behind in mourning.

Ah – those were the days! For indeed fifty years have passed since I first visited Studmarsh. I am but a spectre now, leaning on a broken gate. The shutters of the building have been smashed in. Half the roof is missing and rain tumbles into the empty chamber. I am the Black Death. Decay and disorder are my legacy. I rip up social fabric and toss the rags to the four winds.

As I turn away I spy a drunken cleric slumped on the grass, flagon in his left hand, ripped prayer book in his right. Some of the torn pages are flitting across the meadow like wingless butterflies.

But who really cares? Who has enough stamina to protest? Has anyone even noticed?

Who in Studmarsh is still intact?

I am the Black Death. It's 1397 and decaying Studmarsh is still mine.

A Day in the Life of a Visitor to Studmarsh.

My name and what people call me is Adam Vinetree, and this is the tale of my travels northwest from Dorset (my place of birth) to find work and seek employment. I will undertake any task and put my hands to whatever job will pay enough to shelter me, buy me food and find a wench so that I can finally settle down.

I had tried to settle in many different places, but alas, could not stay long for the Plague ever seemed to be round the corner taking the friends I had in my youth and the few that I had made on my journey. In my experience of work I have cared for livestock, can guide a plough and I learn very quickly. I have sheared sheep and picked up some of the art of the blacksmith, the locals in villages I have passed and stayed in are attracted to the blacksmith for he is the place for talk and news.

I came to a small place of the name of Studmarsh. I entered the village and headed for the plume of smoke and hubbub surrounding one hut. There were a few locals gathered and my eyes were attracted to a pretty young girl who stood out as the most attractive girl I had ever seen! Tearing my eyes away, I pushed through the crowd to talk directly with the big man holding great metal pincers and throwing logs on the fire.

"Scuse me sir, is there anywhere local I can work? I can fetch timbers for the fire, push the bellows and make and repair horse-shoes." I also said to him, "I am new here and need a hot dinner and a place to sleep." The blacksmith stopped what he was doing and scratched his chin. "I can spread the word about, stick around the area and I'll see what I can do."

I thanked him and turned to leave, and there was the beautiful girl I saw earlier, approaching me! She stopped in front of me and said; "Hello, my name is Alice and I overheard your conversation. My Father is looking for an extra man to till our land for grain. I think I could persuade him to let you sleep in the cleaner part of the goat shed, there is plenty of bedding and Daisy is pretty good, even with strangers."

I cannot believe my ears! I know that Alice had not asked her Father yet, but I was quietly confident that I had found a place to work, sleep and the chance of finding a wife within thirty minutes of entering the village!

Alice gave me such a coy look; I could not help but smile. She took my hand and led me through the village to where she pointed to the raised flat area at the top of the valley. There was a large settlement to the right of the track, and Alice told me that this was her home – I could see that this family were not stuck for a coin or two, so we headed for the large gates to the property and as we went to push them open, something caught my eye.

Festooned upon several of the village doors was the dreaded sign of a red cross painted in crude, hurried strokes.

I stood there and took it all in, sure as sure the village was slowly becoming doomed, Alice started to cry in the background, saying "You will stay here with us, won't you?" My heart almost gave way at that point: this girl was at the end of her tether, her risk of infection was almost a certainty. The plague itself was seething through the large towns and settlements and people were dying in no particular order, if I stayed here I would almost certainly succumb to Black Death, if I leave I would never see this pretty a face and the wealth this family had, ever again.

Maybe I stay and barricade Alice and me both in together – maybe I run and die a slow, horrible Death . . .

The Black Death, together with the famines of the preceding decades, took between a third and half the population of Herefordshire, cutting ordinary people off from help, and causing sufferers and communities to build their own barriers for protection. Today it is known that one in four people will suffer mental ill health during their lives. The congruity between these stark figures, and the histories hidden beneath them, led to the writing of **A Day in the Life of One in Four.**

I am someone who happens to be 'one in four'.

I have to fight it now. Today I have an interview for a place at University, but when I try to go out, the front door is no longer a door. It is like a griffin preventing me from leaving the house. If I fight it there will be more of them waiting for me outside. But I want to be an archaeologist, and all the griffins in England won't stop me getting there. I make it outside. There is a cold wind and people walk past me shivering or blowing into their hands. I hold my head down, for I cannot tell if they are friendly or hostile. Someone is talking on their mobile. Does this mean there will be people waiting for me round the corner? Ready to hurt me like they did before – I must change my route. They'll be expecting me to go past the park. I decide to cut through town but this means I have to walk faster, always making sure I keep my head down so no one can catch my eye.

Then it dawns on me that I have forgotten my gloves. I am exposed. I stand out. I am a target. I thrust my hands deep inside my pockets, hoping that no one has seen. Suddenly I hear my name. I spin round, expecting an attack. I am totally defenceless; I shut my eyes and prepare to take a hit. But no one is there, only a river of faceless people. One of these faceless people has been watching me since I left the house. Any minute I might feel a hand on my shoulder or a knife in my back. My heart tries to clamber through my chest. I freeze with fear, and my whole body crawls with cold sweat. "Who called my name?" I call out in panic but no one answers. A few people stare and then edge away from me. I know those surreptitious glances.

They think I am mad. I am a threat to them. I might harm their children. I want to yell out that I am the one who is afraid. I forgot my gloves this morning, I am the one in danger! I've got to get home. I feel outnumbered in this unfriendly town. But my legs are now blocks of wood holding me to the ground.

I scream inside, unable to move forward. I ask a passer-by to call me a taxi but she hurries on, pretending she never heard me. Like other people, she sees my agitation but fails to see the human being inside. No one wants to help me. People are really staring now. I feel so alone in this crowd. I hold my head, unsure what to do. I start willing my body to move from this place. Very, very slowly, I am able to inch forward but I cannot go back the way I came, for it is too dangerous.

Two hours later I am outside my front door. The familiar front door is no longer a griffin but an ally. He pulls me inside and then shields me from the outside world.

I am listening to a message on my answer-phone informing me that as I failed to make my interview they cannot offer me a University place. The caller wishes me well and adds that I may apply again in a year's time.

Abigail Biddle, daughter of Richard and Mary, was the lady whose marriage we could not find, no matter where we searched. She was the elusive 'other', who reminded us not to put people into neat pigeon holes and categories. Did she marry for love? Or to escape from home? Why did her brother never marry? Was he looking after his widowed mother, or was she caring for him, long after he had reached adulthood? **A Day in the Life of Abigail** stands for all the unrevealed complexities in people we think we know.

My name is Abigail. I flutter through time, passing through Studmarsh from age to age. One moment I am picking flowers in the meadow. Next I am watching through an upstairs window; watching you. You are trying to capture me, but I am the elusive Abigail.

Elusive Abigail, I run through Studmarsh tossing my hair and laughing as it glistens in the golden light.

Then I am wailing, for my father has just died in his bed. This is grieving Abigail.

This is a finely dressed Abigail drowned in a black cape of loss. The Abigail who makes you shudder on a windswept night at the thought of ghosts. Yes, I am that ghost you thought you saw by the oak tree. Yet before you catch me I am galloping away on a black-maned mare, breaking through time into new pastures.

It is my wedding day now. Listen to the pealing bells! This is time for more laughter on Studmarsh. Perhaps on a summer evening you might hear me making merry just as I did on that joyful day.

I am the woman who holds all the memories. They are my secrets.

If you listen carefully you may hear whispers in the water. Bond's Dingle or the watery marsh - who knows? Elusive Abigail likes to tease. She jumps out and surprises you. She lies in dusty books then runs away when you open the page. Abigail flies through time, neither young nor old. You think you know her, but you merely know her name. Abigail: "joy of my father".

I am elusive Abigail, the unknown woman of Studmarsh. You will never catch me, for you will never know me. Strange, as I am standing right behind you, giggling because you're reluctant to turn round.

If we came to see Abigail as a reminder of the futility of categorising people, so the project participants also appreciated ever more fully the hidden talents in each other – whether it was good humour in the terrible weather, artistic ability

76

or language skills. **A Day in the Life of a Blind Storyteller** celebrated this. Moreover, it celebrated the opportunity for a disabled person to make a unique contribution to their community.

> That winter of 1435 I saw the trees standing tall and stark, but I never saw them glisten in the spring. For many months I lay in a fever, caught between heaven and earth in a world of ice and fire. Many people would arrive with baskets of herbs and leave with the smell of death lingering on their clothes.

> It is said that Robert the cleric begged the Lord Jesus to carry me away in his arms, for he could not bear to hear my cries of anguish. But the Lord Jesus shook his head and sent an Angel to sit beside me. When the fever finally left me, I woke to find my eyes in darkness.

> Such a darkness it was, that it left a cold imprint on my soul. It is true that I cursed my fate, and some believed I was born of the Devil. But what the Lord takes away with one hand, He gives with another.

> I was given the freedom to wander into many different worlds, and a tongue to describe my adventures. You are trapped in a world where trees have green leaves and brown trunks. But I see trees in thousands of different colours. You have to travel on foot or by horse. But I have wings that let me fly. I can go anywhere without moving from this room.

> Travellers come from afar to hear my tales. They bring baskets of bread, or kindle for the fire. Even when melancholia steals my wings, I find herbs and fruit outside my door. When I feel my wings pinned once more against my back ready for another journey, the colours I see are even brighter and the lands I visit are more enchanting.

> Many people ask me what it is like to be blind. But I reply that I am not blind, for I see far more than they do.

The Past in Mind project generated new skills, new confidence and new belief in what is possible. Just as the literate Colleys and Biddles of Studmarsh were empowered far beyond their unlettered contemporaries, so Past in Mind freed people to make new marks in the world. **A Day in the Life of 'Making our Mark'.**

> Waddling…walking…sensing…seeing.
> Reading the landscape. Orientation.
> Plotting out the markers in the field.
> Maps… patterns…perspectives.
> Changes …indicators … base lines.

> Angles of photos taken, from the North, the South, the sky above.
> Degrees… minutes… seconds.

> The protractor moves by my hand – yes my hand! (*Suddenly, and for the first time I know how to navigate the world*)

Clayey…silty… grainy… brown – no, brown with reddish tints
Colours, hues… (*I'd never noticed or known how to notice until now.*)

Taste it… feel it… sense it.

Context… bedding planes… bedrock… 'getting your eye in' as Dai would say…
Make a mark…make a judgement… watch the trowel… gently does it.
Sparkling quartz-like shiny, tiny sharks' teeth or little baby milk teeth - looking up at us from the soil.

Walls emerge, doorways too?
Now walking, not waddling, respectfully through peoples' front rooms… seeing their crockery sensing their lives.
What did they eat? High/low/middle fortune in life?
Did they 'keep up with the Joneses'? Did they grow up with their husbands-to-be?
Did the fields feel as long and treacherous, come winter or summer?
How far was 'far' to them?

Did they have the same dreams – see the next parish, town, county – or were they too bogged down by life and making ends meet?
Did the plague come knocking?
Boggy, uneven, hard to till land, that today sees cattle graze, so warm & peacefully.

They left us their horse shoes, cooking pots – blackened in production & from making wholesome, hard-toiled-for, food for their precious families. Nails, glass, sherds, such 'treasures' that saw so much life & passed down through the years and generations.

Did they experience the same emotional 'rush' when they found something washed, exposed by rain and brook – nestling the pieces of their ancestors' lives, treasuring, dreaming…? Reworking them, knowing how precious they were to their makers, and knowing that such things should never be discarded lightly.

They will never be forgotten, they have made their mark in a settlement that will now never pass out of history because of what they have shared so preciously with us. They have made their mark and we the volunteers of Past in Mind have made a mark and it has made a mark on us!

Above all, Past in Mind was about a group of people, who came together first as strangers, wary of each other, uncertain who was who. And we grew together as we learnt, and we had fun. And we came to understand a little of each other, and a little of the lives of the other people of Studmarsh, from times past. **A Day in the life of Richard Biddle.**

We are a mongrel race, we English. Our blood comes from the ancient Celts who first fought and then greeted the armies of Rome. It comes from the Angles and the Saxons who took land here when the legions had gone. It comes from the ferocious Danes who ravaged our villages and monasteries and it comes from the all-conquering Normans. Our native tongue brays our heritage every time we speak it.

And do you know what? I am proud to be a mongrel. I am proud to be a Herefordshire man. I am proud to be a Biddle.

The Whitbourne parson tells me that my forebears are buried there for five generations, and I know lying deep in that rich earth there are more. The monkish records survived the sad self-slaughter of Cromwell and Charles and tell me that an Angle named Bita claimed land here over a thousand years ago. Could he be my ancestor? Bita – Bidda – Biddle. The chameleon names mutate with the centuries, but the rich blood flows from generation to generation, carrying our love-of-land with it. We ARE the land. We ARE the soil. We ARE England. I am Richard Biddle, of the Studmarsh Biddles and I drink to your health!

They say we lost a hundred thousand men in the Civil War. It was madness upon madness. The arrogance of a king who deemed himself un-needy of consent - the ferociousness of the New Model Army of Fairfax and Cromwell, who taught Charles that the people are the land, not he - the sieges, the mass battles, the starvation, the disease. Our land bled and wept and some left it to its fate. Some profited from it in the buying of land cheaply from those devastated by the fighting. Some even of my own country-folk took their money to Jamaica and turned African sweat and Caribbean rain into tobacco and sugary gold.

But not the Biddles! We stayed where we'd always been, amongst the rich meadows, the tench-filled streams and the fruitful orchards that nourished the apples which made the cider for my ancient tankard. Your health! Oh, we payed the war-tax and we fed the troops when they were billeted close by, and we sang the Lilly Bulero with them round their camp fires. But we stayed put, where we'd always been and neither the hell of the Black Death, nor the threat of invasion from Spain, nor the brother-on-brother blood-letting could drive us off this land from which our bones are made. We ARE Studmarsh and if you cut my body in two, you would find the name of it written inside of me, just like the trinkets of the merchants.

So what of the future? Will the Biddles still be here five hundred years hence? Will some future Richard Biddle stand upon this stage and tell you he is a Studmarsh Biddle and damned proud of it? I tell you YES. He will have seen more wars and more famines and more emigrations and he will speak in a different accent, but he will drink the same Studmarsh cider from the same Studmarsh tankard that I raise to you now – YOUR HEALTH!

Bibliography

Archive Sources

Bromyard and District Local History Society (BDLHS): copies of parish registers and documents including wills, The Red Book and Swithin Butterfield's Survey.

Hereford Record Office (HRO): copies of parish registers and originals of wills, The Red Book and Swithin Butterfield's Survey.

Public Record Office: on-line access to Canterbury will of Thomas Jones, 1720.

Secondary Sources

Anon, 'Notes from the Winter Annual Meeting, 1932', *Transactions of the Woolhope Naturalists' Field Club* 1930-1932 (1935): xcix.

Atkin, C.W, 'Herefordshire' in *The Domesday Geography of Midland England*, ed. H.C Darby and I.B Terrett (2 edn; Cambridge: Cambridge University Press, 1971): 57-114.

Bailey, M, 'The Concept of the Margin in the Medieval English Economy', *The Economic History Review* New Series 42 (1989): 1-17.

Baring-Gould, S, and J Fisher, ed., *The Lives of the British Saints* (2 edn; Felinfach: Llanerch Facsimile Reprints, 2000).

Barker, P, ed., *From Roman Viroconium to Medieval Wroxeter: Recent Work on the Site of the Roman City of Wroxeter* (Worcester: West Mercian Archaeological Consultants Limited, 1990).

Capes, W W, ed., *Registrum Ricardi De Swinfield, Episcopi Herefordensis A.D. 1283-1317* (2 vols.; The Registers of the Bishops of Hereford; Hereford: Canterbury and York Society, 1909).

Capes, W W, ed., *Registrum Johanes Trefnant, Episcopi Herefordensis A.D. 1389-1404* (The Registers of the Bishops of Hereford; Hereford: Canterbury and York Society, 1916).

Children, G, and G Nash, *A Guide to Prehistoric Sites in Herefordshire* (Monuments in the Landscape; Leominster: Logaston Press, 1994).

Coplestone-Crow, B, *Herefordshire Place Names* (2 edn; Leominster: Logaston Press, 2009).

Davies, J, 'Herefordshire', *Transactions of the Woolhope Naturalists' Field Club* 1900-1902 (1902): 248-84.

Dohar, W J, *The Black Death and Pastoral Leadership: The Diocese of Hereford in the Fourteenth Century* (Philadelphia: University of Pennsylvania Press, 1995).

Fenwick, C C, ed., *The Poll Taxes of 1377, 1379 and 1381: Part 1 Bedfordshire - Leicestershire* (Records of Social and Economic History; Oxford: The British Academy, 1998).

Galbraith, V H, and J Tait, ed., *Herefordshire Domesday, Circa 1160-1170* (The Pipe Roll Society; London: 1950).

Gelling, M, *Signposts to the Past: Place-Names and the History of England* (third edn; Chichester: Phillimore, 1997).

——, *The West Midlands in the Early Middle Ages*, ed. N Brooks (Studies in the Early History of Britain; Leicester: Leicester University Press, 1992).

Grant, M, ed., *Tacitus: The Annals of Imperial Rome* (Penguin Classics; London: Penguin, 2003).

Griffiths, R G, ed., *Registrum Thome De Cantilupo, Episcopi Herefordensis A.D. 1275-1282* (2 vols.; The Registers of the Bishops of Hereford; Hereford: Canterbury and York Society, 1906).

Hanks, P, et al., ed., *The Oxford Names Companion: The Definitive Guide to Surnames, First Names and Place Names of the British Isles* (Oxford: Oxford University Press, 2002).

Hartley, L P, *The Go-Between* (London: Penguin, 1953).

Hooke, D, 'Anglo-Saxon Landscapes of the West Midlands: The Charter Evidence' in *B.A.R. British* (1981).

Kiddey, R, and J Schofield, 'Embrace the Margins: Adventures in Archaeology and Homelessness', *Public Archaeology* 10 (2011): 4-22.

Kneen, A, 'Who Was Swithin Butterfield?' *Bromyard and District Local History Society Journal* 33 (2011): 11-13.

McClure, J, and R Collins, ed., *Bede: The Ecclesiastical History of the English People, the Greater Chronicle and Bede's Letter to Egbert* (Oxford: Oxford University Press, 1969).

Moore, J S, 'The Mid-Tudor Population Crisis in Midland England, 1548-1563', *Midland History* 34 (2009): 44-57.

Parry, J H, ed., *Registrum Johanes De Trilleck, Episcopi Herefordensis A.D. 1344-1361* (2 vols.; The Registers of the Bishops of Hereford; Hereford: Canterbury and York Society, 1910).

——, ed., *Registrum Roberti Mascall, Episcopi Herefordensis A.D. 1404-1417* (The Registers of the Bishops of Hereford; Hereford: Canterbury and York Society, 1917).

Ratkai, S, 'Pottery Report ' in *Studmarsh Medieval Settlement, Brockhampton, Herefordshire*, ed. D Williams and C Atkinson (Hereford: Herefordshire Archaeology, 2012): 44-47.

Rivet, A.L.F, and C Smith, *The Place Names of Roman Britain* (London: Batsford, 1979).

Royal College of Psychiatrists, Social Inclusion Scoping Group, 'Making Psychiatry and Mental Health Services Fit for the 21st Century: Mental Health and Social Inclusion' (2009) <www.rcpsych.ac.uk/pdf/Ps01_2009x.pdf>.

Shoesmith, R, 'The Western Rampart', *Transactions of the Woolhope Naturalists' Field Club* 39 (1967): 51-67.

Skingley, P, ed., *Coins of England and the United Kingdom* (41 edn; London: Spink and Son Ltd, 2006).

Slavin, P, 'The Great Bovine Pestilence and Its Economic and Environmental Consequences in England and Wales, 1318-50', *The Economic History Review* 65 (2012): 1239-66.

Stanford, S.C, 'The Deserted Medieval Village of Hampton Wafer, Herefordshire', *Transactions of the Woolhope Naturalists' Field Club* 39 (1967): 71-92.

Swanton, M, ed., *Anglo-Saxon Prose* (2nd edn; London: J.M.Dent, 1993).

Thirsk, J, *Alternative Agriculture: A History from the Black Death to the Present Day* (Oxford: Oxford University Press, 1997).

Vince, A, 'Did They Use Pottery in the Welsh Marches and the West Midlands between the Fifth and Twelfth Centuries A.D.?' in *From Roman Town to Norman Castle: Essays in Honour of Philip Barker*, ed. A Burl (Birmingham: Birmingham University Press, 1988): 40-55.

Weale, J, *A History of Tedstone Delamere, in North-East Herefordshire* (Bromyard: Bromyard and District Local History Society, 2013).

Webster, G, 'A Trial Trench across the Defences of the Roman Fort at Tedstone Wafer, Herefordshire', *Transactions of the Woolhope Naturalists' Field Club* 34 (1954): 284-87.

Whitelock, D, *English Historical Documents 500-1042* (2 edn; London and New York: Routledge, 1979).

Whiteman, A, and M Clapinson, ed., *The Compton Census of 1676: A Critical Edition* (Records of Social and Economic History, N.S.; London: Oxford University Press, for The British Academy, 1986).

Williams, A, and G H Martin, ed., *Domesday Book: A Complete Translation* (2 edn; London: Penguin, 2003).

Williams, D, and C Atkinson, 'Studmarsh Medieval Settlement, Brockhampton, Herefordshire: A Summary Report on Excavations in August 2012' in *Herefordshire Archaeology Reports* (Hereford: Herefordshire Archaeology, 2013).

Williams, P, *Bromyard: Minster, Manor and Town* (Bromyard: Bromyard and District Local History Society, 1987).

——, *Whitbourne, a Bishop's Manor* (Bromyard: Bromyard and District Local History Society, 1979).

Winterbottom, M, ed., *Gildas: The Ruin of Britain, and Other Documents* (History from the Sources; Chichester: Phillimore and Co. Ltd., 1978).

Zaluckyj, S, *Mercia: The Anglo-Saxon Kingdom of Central England* (2 edn; Leominster: Logaston Press, 2011).